To Eileen -
with Love -
Christina Thomas

ALSO BY CHRISTINA THOMAS

SECRETS: A Practical Guide to Undreamed-of Possibilities

IN

TUNE

WITH THE

SOUL

Christina Thomas

For Information on Workshops and Seminars
by Christina Thomas, write or call:

 Inner Light Institute
C/o The Publisher

Publisher:

Chela Publications
977 Seminole Trail, Suite 308
Charlottesville, VA 22901 • USA

Publisher's Cataloging in Publication
(Prepared by Quality Books Inc.)

Thomas, Christina
    In Tune With The Soul / Christina Thomas
    p. cm.
    Includes bibliographical references and index.
    ISBN 0-9622119-4-X

1. New Age movement. 2. Spiritual life. I. Title.

BP605.N48T6 1992   299.93
                                        QB192-569

1 2 3 4 5 6 7 8 9 0

Dedicated
to
Love

ACKNOWLEDGEMENTS

I am grateful for love, support and encouragement from many people during the writing of this book, especially:

Richard Garretson, for love and support which is always free of condition.

Laura Ward, for hours of devoted editing and other assistance.

My Beloved Julie, for understanding when I was writing "all the time."

William Thomas, for your indomitable humor and loving heart.

Linda Levy, for your aliveness, faith and unconditional love.

Zulma X. Barrios, for your strength and love.

Priya Hossack, for holding me in the light and love of the One.

Jan Tober, for your love and laughter.

Angelo and Marge DeVivo, Benini and Lorraine Benini, Tom and Holly Wharton, Elaine Heroux, Marilyn McWilliams, Mac Bush and Maggie Webb Adams. Thank you for your love and support.

To the clients and workshop participants with whom I learn so much: Thank you for the courage to "go for the gold" in your own lives.

And to the Beloved nonphysical Ones who woke me all those pre-dawn mornings to write, and whose ecstatic vibrations reverberate throughout these pages, I thank you for love, light and learning.

May my life be like the banks of a river, channeling the mighty, surging flow of Divine Love to thirsty souls.

In Tune With The Soul
by Christina Thomas

Contents

Please Read This

Throughout this book I have primarily used the masculine gender when it seems to flow more easily. The English language has no really comfortable, non-gender pronoun for the third person. A writer or speaker could use "one" but it sometimes sounds tired and using "he and/or she" feels clumsy to me, whether I am the writer or reader!

Regarding the use of pronouns to refer to God or the Divine: God is a spirit, an energy, a force which is beyond any physical form and certainly beyond any gender. Technically, the most accurate words might be to refer to God as "the great unmanifest beyond creation," but that becomes *truly* cumbersome, so sometimes I use "He," intending also to include "She." I, personally, think of God as Divine Mother as frequently as any other aspect. And *any* concept of God is just a way to think about one aspect or expression of the Divine and, therefore, is very limited.

So I ask you to stretch and bend with me as you read this book; please don't let the words get in the way. I could simply have said, "Use of the masculine gender is acknowledged; thank you for letting it be." But today there are many struggles — for more equal women's rights, which I wholeheartedly support, and the very real struggles of males to individuate themselves, also — and many people have become sensitized by these struggles. If you can read through the words in this book to feel the spirit beyond, the highest good will be served, for ultimately, whether you are in a male or a female body, the real quest is to transcend any limited identity in order to be In Tune With The Soul.

A Letter to My Readers

Very young children are natural and spontaneous. It is usually pretty easy to know how they feel because they *let* you know, honestly and without delay. By adulthood, however, most learn to keep the innermost self somewhat hidden. Because of this, the interior life becomes a secret world. If one is lucky, he remembers how to find his way back to this sanctuary, even if he can take no one else with him. It is more common, however, to forget the existence of this magical place. As this amnesia sets in, he loses much of the ability to interact with the love and power emanating from his most sacred inner self and his happiness diminishes accordingly.

My most thrilling discoveries have been those that helped me return to this childlike contentment. The inner world I now experience is my greatest treasure and I feel centered and happy most of the time. Like a boundless ocean full of life-giving water, it is, for me, a place of happy adventure, the most complete safety and the sweetest bliss. I feel enormously grateful for this spiritual dimension in my life. Rather than a blessing, I count it as *the* blessing.

When I observe turmoil in people's lives, I suspect that they are experiencing inner pain, for hurtful behavior does not originate from spiritual peace. If long years have elapsed since you were as happy as a little one, you may feel a bit overwhelmed at even the thought of sorting through all the debris which may be scattered over the terrain of a lifetime.

"I long for the freedom and joy I felt as a child," people sometimes say, "but I don't know how to start reclaiming it." When I hear such longing, I sometimes think of a beach littered with thousands of shreds of trash and imagine one person out there with a garbage bag attempting to clean up the mess piece by piece. All of a sudden one huge wave crashes onto shore and, when it recedes back into the sea, the entire beach is as beautifully clean as if the fragments never existed, and that individual is standing there soaking wet and laughing. This is what it feels like to come into contact with the ocean of divine love — one big wave washes onto your life and begins carrying the particles of illusion away.

It is as though that ocean is our home, anyway, but long ago we walked out onto the shore to lie in the sun for a while, then wandered further inland and forgot where home was. With time, we began to feel really dried out, thirsting for relief. We meet others in the same predicament, perhaps attending classes filled with such people, all seeking a remedy for dehydration. All we actually need do to heal our maladies, however, is go back home to the ocean. The next question we usually ask is, "How, specifically, do I find my way back?" While there is more than one route that will lead you to it, a good rule of thumb is to ask someone who already lives there to escort you to the water's edge.

Society's requirement that we keep to ourselves is somewhat binding on all of us. My work as an author and metaphysical teacher gives me the opportunity to bypass some restrictions and share this indwelling bliss with others. I have written about very numinous experiences here, which have been powerfully rejuvenating and transforming for me. Occasionally I share them verbally in workshops and listeners say that they feel greatly uplifted, as I hope you will. If the descriptions of some of them seem unusual or startling at first, you may wish to think about them as if they are dreams.

If you truly hear my story as you read on, it is a gift to me. If you also begin to reopen your own sanctuary and remember how to be as joyful as a little child, then it is a magnificent gift to both of us. I know that if you receive real, practical benefit from this book, it is not because the words are perfect but because the divine energy of the soul is present as it is written. So, as you read, if you feel a response from within, it is, perhaps, your soul resonating to wisdom it already knows, to joy it already feels and to rhythm it already dances.

Millions of people are born, live and die without ever glimpsing the true purpose of their lives. As we move through these pages together, it is my heart's desire that a word or a thought or the energy which enlivens it will lead you to be In Tune With The Soul.

Namaste,

Christina

1

A Thread of Ecstasy

Many people struggle to feel okay about themselves.
When you finally awaken to a true experience of the
light of your own soul, what you will discover is:
You're not just okay; you're magnificent!
Christina Thomas

There is a beautiful park near my home. I go there to walk
sometimes among the many towering, deciduous trees. On
a cool, misty day at the end of autumn, a remarkable experience occurred. Here are my journal notes:

Just as I arrive beneath a huge, old oak whose
nearly-bare branches stretch protectingly in all directions, my attention quickly shifts from my primary purpose of getting exercise amidst the natural
beauty of the park to the intense love suddenly
bursting out from my heart center and spreading
throughout my body, making me feel like I am
melting. I feel less separate than when I began my
walk a few minutes ago. The form of my body is still
separate but the essence of my being exists everywhere. I look up through the branches of a tree and
feel the same sweetness playing in the breeze and
the leaves softly blowing in the wind. This is God —
the presence of God — so near, so available, so
present everywhere.

This experience is not a surprise to me for it happens frequently. I know it to be the ecstatic expansion into the fourth-dimensional energy of boundless, unconditional love. In this state I feel perfect peace, perfect joy, utter contentment. I feel love for everything and everyone — not as a philosophical concept — but a tremendous moving, surging bliss that dissolves my egoistic boundaries.

I am aware that most people do not experience such ecstasy or even know of its existence, though greater numbers of people are now awakening to it. The seed of divine love, which has long been planted, resides in the soul of each person and will burst into conscious awareness when conditions are right to bring forth the blossom.

Once the remarkable awakening process begins in an individual, wonderful life changes begin to occur, including the advent of a deep sense of well-being and spiritual peace. A dynamic shift in energy leaves him feeling suddenly lighter and younger and is immediately observable in the eyes. The gaze becomes soft, unguarded, powerfully intense and appears to burn with love once the inner floodgates are opened to allow free flow to the long pent-up spiritual waters. Observing such an awakened one, it is easy to understand why the eyes are called the "windows of the soul." Sometimes I observe this loving energy spread like a magnificent contagion to others. Certainly it is what all are seeking, for finding this love, one has found home.

What is this awakening? How does it occur? Why does it happen to one person and not another? In my own life, the awareness of this spiritual energy has been present from my earliest memories. From the time I was a small child, I asked many philosophical questions: Who am I? What am I looking for? What will make me happy? What is the purpose of life on earth, anyway? The outer world seemed less real to me somehow, compared to the inner world of energy in which I lived.

This inner kingdom was filled with a living presence, which sometimes spoke to me, giving guidance and know-ingness. At other times it took the form of visible inner light or I felt it in the body kinesthetically. Although it did not prevent painful, traumatic events in my outer world, the inner place always felt comforting and reassuring. I did not realize then that my experience was unusual and, indeed, I still believe that it is natural in most children. For whatever reason, my awareness and ability to feel these energies, to hear the inner voice and see the spiritual light did not atrophy as it apparently does in most people.

As I grew into adolescence, however, I became less content than I had been in childhood; I felt more alone and my inner searching became more urgent. One day in my freshman year of high school - I was 14 years old - an inner connection was made with Jesus that was powerful and numinous. This was something that just happened, for I had not known to seek such an experience. I spoke of it to no one, but from that moment on, I felt less alone. Difficulties which had character-ized my adolescent behavior until then abruptly ceased. I felt less need to rebel because I felt more love and contentment inside and had more clarity about my direction in life.

Even though this inward experience was very significant to me, outer everyday events were no worse or better than in most other lives and I imagine that my life would have seemed unremarkable to any outside observer. I now realize, however, that something extraordinarily remarkable was occurring all along. Like a sparkling, clear, underground river surges powerfully on its course, unseen above ground but relentlessly carving its way through every obstacle, my soul was doing its glorious, hidden work, unimpeded by the mundane dramas of the years. I could not have used these words to describe my experience then, but it was as though a thread of ecstasy was weaving a brilliant color into the fabric of my life which made everything else look drab by comparison.

Unable to find sufficient meaning in the material values of the world around me, I kept questioning and searching. In 1971 that search led me to "Autobiography of a Yogi," a classic of spiritual literature by Paramahansa Yogananda, wherein I first consciously learned of a very great spiritual master known as Mahavatar Babaji. It was Babaji, Yogananda said, who secretly had inspired the lives of many great people, including his own. Babaji had, in fact, chosen Yogananda to journey from India to America to spread the teachings of the liberating science of Kriya Yoga.

By 1973 I had qualified to receive initiation into Kriya Yoga and traveled to Los Angeles for that purpose. The Initiation Ceremony at the Mother Center was held that year on my birthday, July 12th. Throughout the long evening service, I had my first experience of what I have come to call "dual consciousness." I was aware that my body was on Mount Washington in Los Angeles and that the monk officiating was Brother Mokshananda, but in my inward experience, which seemed more real somehow, I was on Drongiri Mountain in the Himalayas and the initiation was being conducted by none other than Babaji. I felt a total surrender to this great Being and the purest, most outrageous amount of love for Him. Indeed, I felt intoxicated with a spiritual ecstasy more intense than anything I had ever known. The experience lasted throughout the evening and the bus trip back down the mountain with the other initiates. I felt indescribable joy and peace. It was 2:00 a.m. by the time I fell asleep in my room at the Biltmore Hotel.

At 5:00 o'clock the next morning, without a wake-up call, I sat up in bed, wide awake. The moment my spine became vertical, I felt a sensation like an oil - intensely warm and radiantly alive - was being poured from the top of my head down my spine to its base. Simultaneously, the exhilaration of the previous night returned full force. This ecstatic state lasted until some time later that day when I began to feel more like my normal self. At the end of the week, I returned to my home in Chicago and continued to follow the spiritual path set out by Yogananda and Babaji, with a primary focus on daily practice of Kriya Yoga meditation.

Two years later my daughter was born at Michael Reese Hospital. Although the pregnancy had been easy, complications set in during labor. After the first twelve hours, my body was gripped with contractions of energy so intense it was difficult to breathe correctly, but at the same time I felt such divine love that the overall experience was one of bliss. I could feel the presence of Yogananda, Christ, Babaji and other non-physical beings in the labor room with me. It was as though a huge window from heaven opened and remained open throughout the twenty hours of labor. The first glimpse of my baby's face was a look into the eyes of an angel. She did not cry (though I did), but gazed into my eyes with a depth and power directly from the soul.

She was only three years old when an even more graphic experience of dual consciousness occurred. My husband had a massive stroke. In a coma, he was connected by numerous wires to machines and monitors in the Intensive Care Unit. His doctors had prepared me for the worst; his death seemed imminent. My heart was broken, my mind reeling under the weight of belief that my child had lost her father and I had lost my beloved spouse. It felt like my human life was in shambles around my feet. Again, however, I felt surrounded and buoyed by the non-physical presences of Babaji, Christ and Yogananda, and an attendant blissful awareness so full of love that its intensity actually competed with the anguish. I even heard devotional bhajans which were very uplifting to me and, while I knew that this was an inward experience and that others in the ICU could not hear the soothing music, it, nevertheless, sounded to me like a radio playing nearby. So once again I was blessed by an inward attunement to a very high plane of spiritual peace while my conscious mind was undergoing painful and difficult circumstances.

One day during Bill's long hospital confinement, I found myself thinking about a phenomenon which was occurring with increasing frequency: With all the grief I felt about his condition, I also noticed that I felt a lot of love for almost everyone at the hospital, including the medical staff, the other patients, people in the cafeteria and the orderly who mopped the floor. I had been in love with God for a long time; now it seemed I was in love with people, too. Suddenly it occurred to me that this expansion of the heart's love was an aspect of Superconsciousness and I said to God, "Is *this* how you do it? A tragedy comes along like a wrecking ball to shatter the heart - - and then the heart expands to love far more than it was capable of before." It felt like God shrugged huge shoulders and quipped, "It works!"

I realized in that moment that, faced with a life event of overwhelming intensity such as I was experiencing, there were two choices only: (a) Feel the pain, expand the consciousness and love more or (b) reject the experience, refuse to feel the pain and become bitter. I felt grateful that I had been able to fully experience this part of my life, which was as rich as it was painful.

A few years later, I sold our home and was moving with my daughter to Encinitas, California, to live near Yogananda's ashram. Another experience of dual consciousness occurred, which I can relate best, perhaps, by sharing my journal notes:

I have signed the transit slip and the huge moving van has pulled away with all our belongings inside. Chicago has been home for many years. . . and tomorrow my 6-year-old Julie and I will leave here forever. Alone now, I lean against the wall of the garage and feel drained and sad.

I head back inside for one last time, back into the home I have loved more than any other this lifetime. As I walk through each lovely room, now denuded of furniture and waiting hauntingly for me, I allow scenes from the past to replay: the prettiest Christmas tree we ever had looked so festive in this graceful living room. And in this sunny bedroom, a baby crib held our precious little one as she grew from infant to toddler, and was replaced by pretty white furniture during her pre-school years.

The master bedroom, once our comfortable nest, became a convalescent's room when I brought my husband home from the hospital after the stroke. Each room holds its ghosts, its bittersweet memories.

Faced with saying a final goodbye to this familiar place, I feel virtually torn apart with grief and great heaving sobs arise in wave after wave from my insides. I move through

the rooms moaning like an animal, grateful to
be alone and allow the grieving. But as painful
as it is, it also feels like swimming in a vast
ocean of aliveness and love. For grief this
searing only comes with love very deep.

I look back on the years I have lived in
Chicago and ask myself: "What would I change
if I could live all these years over again?"

The answer is swift and certain: "I would
love more, love better, love all the time and
never find a reason to withhold love."

Later, while living in California, the healing process in my
own life accelerated tremendously. The years of Kriya Yoga
and meditation had prepared me to move rapidly in awareness and I made many new discoveries. I devoted time to
alternative methods of empowerment and healing.

Of the various approaches with which I experimented, one
of the most significant shifts in energy came in 1981 with my
first session of connected breathing. During the initial, very
powerful, experience, I re-lived several childhood events
which had been the source of some early pain. I wept, feeling
sadness and a mixture of many other emotions. I was entirely
present on the inside of myself somehow, where past experiences remained alive and intact. The hour of gentle, connected breathing culminated in my feeling that I had a baby
in my womb and, simultaneously, that I was the baby being

born* These images, of course, make no sense in any ordinary, third-dimensional way of thinking, but this altered state is quite extraordinary, occurring in the timelessness of the fourth dimension. Afterward, I felt happier, more aligned with myself and relieved of an emotional weight I had not known I was carrying.

Encouraged by the impact of this first experience, I began a series of rebirthing sessions which spanned about 18 months. Much more psychological and emotional integration resulted and I realized that this breathing method was a tool I wanted to offer other people. I began my training to become a Professional Rebirther.

---

*This sort of experience occurs so frequently during a person's initial experience that this form of connected breathing is often referred to as "rebirthing." It assists the breather to consciously move more fully into his body, personality and emotions and clear away accumulations of physical, emotional and psychological energy stored since (or even before) conception. This clearing facilitates the opening to the ecstatic energy of the soul in much the same way a door at the end of a corridor can open once an accumulation of baggage is removed.

Kriya Yoga employs a different method of connected breathing to greatly speed up the completion of one's karma. It is a powerful, spiritual technique which helps the meditating devotee to lift his consciousness beyond body, personality, mind and emotions to a high spiritual plane of meditation on the divine.

Connected Breathing as used in rebirthing has a different purpose and result than that achieved by the Kriya breath, and the two methods of connected breathing are different. Having been a Kriyaban (Kriya Yogi) for almost ten years at the time of my first rebirthing experience, I had an immediate intuitive understanding of how the rebirthing process works. For me, it fits with Kriya Yoga like hand in glove. One technique does not replace the other; each operates differently and in a different realm to rapidly clear away obstacles to psycho-spiritual evolution. Just as a person with a toothache will be able to more effectively apply himself to any endeavor if he obtains relief through good dental treatment, I experienced that healing the emotional, mental and psychological levels through rebirthing supported my meditations and practice of Kriya Yoga. (For information regarding Kriya Yoga, you may contact Self-Realization Fellowship in Los Angeles.)

The months spent in Rebirthing School were deeply healing and fast-paced and I felt Babaji's presence with increasing frequency and intensity. But this training was nearly
over when I discovered that others in the rebirthing movement knew of Him, too. For me, this discovery was like
meeting myself all over again. Ten years' practice of Kriya
Yoga had already transformed my life immeasurably. Babaji,
the great Babaji, who had resurrected this ancient technique
and reintroduced it to the world in 1861 and with whom I had
my potent first experience during Kriya Yoga Initiation, was
also present as a divine stimulus in this other form of connected breathing, which now would become a significant
element of my spiritual service. I was stunned to discover
this synchronicity. At the same time it felt perfectly natural.
The lenses of my world were aligning with a powerful,
singular focus, and with that focus came an ecstasy beyond
anything I had ever imagined.

Somebody observed with good humor that when you are
looking for something, it will always be in the last place you
look. This is perfectly understandable, for once you have
found what you are seeking, the search is over. When I
review my life's journey now, I realize that all I ever wanted
was attunement with my soul. This conscious realization of
essential divinity is the ultimate discovery and the searching
ends. The primary focus of life, now, is service to others and
the deepening of self-realization. Frantic and restless no
longer, this journey is one of joy.

All human life
revolves around one supreme truth
and it is this: the all-powerful spirit
which formed universes upon universes
whirling in space
is your essence, too!
The power at the very core of your being
is the omnipotent power behind all creation.
Before you entered the womb of your mother
to begin forming
your present physical body,
you were a ray of light energy,
a piece of consciousness,
floating in space.
That light energy is synonymous with love —
not the counterfeit emotional interactions
which pass for love
among most people —
but love which is an omnipotent force
permeating everything.
The stuff of which you are made
is soul stuff;
your very essence
is love!

2

The Supreme Truth

There are two kinds of people in the world:
Those who have found the love of the soul
and those who are still searching for it.
Christina Thomas

Imagine that somewhere there is a vast, unknown ocean. A ladleful of water is dipped out of that ocean and poured into a cup. Let us say that the water in the ocean is called "God" and the water in the cup is called "soul." The soul, a portion of that divine essence, is pure God consciousness itself, but is individuated, like the water is a *cup* of water as long as it is in a container separate from the ocean. I wonder if this image occurred to the Psalmist David, prompting him to cry with joy: "My cup runneth over." (Psalms 23:5)

All human life revolves around one supreme truth and it is this: the all-powerful spirit which formed universes upon universes whirling in space is your essence, too! The power at the very core of your being is the omnipotent power behind all creation. Before you entered the fertilized cell in the womb of your mother to begin forming your present physical body, you were a ray of light energy, a piece of consciousness, floating in space. That light energy is synonymous with love — not the counterfeit emotional interactions which pass for love among most people — but love which is an omnipotent force permeating everything. The stuff of

which you are made is soul stuff; your very essence is love!
Sathya Sai Baba, a great spiritual master who lives in South
India says:

> *"Know that you are God and from that state you have
> become a human being. Eventually you will go back to
> your source. Do not regard God as something separate
> and distinct from you. God is very much within you."*

Now if you are like most people on earth who are experiencing lack, illness, loneliness or other suffering, you may
already be thinking that this book does not apply to your life.
Please read on, however, for answers follow which will make
sense. If, indeed, you find yourself in painful circumstances,
then you are not experiencing love in your life but are living
in your own kind of hell! The very word "hell" comes from
the Old English word *"helan"* meaning "to wall off, to hide."
When you are walled off from direct contact with your soul,
you are walled off from part of your own self and you will
experience life as a kind of hell. Inasmuch as you identify
yourself as a skin-encapsulated ego separated from the
greater life of the soul, to that extent you are hiding from your
true self.*

*Another word for skin is "hide!" You are *hiding* when you think you are your
physical body, which is covered with hide. It is amusing to see this play on words
woven into language. "Who knows my grammar knows God!" said Panini, great
philologist and Sanskrit scholar of ancient India. When I first read this quotation
twenty years ago, I was truly puzzled. "What in the world does grammar or
language have to do with knowing God?" I wondered, clearly realizing I did not
understand its meaning. As time goes by, however, understanding grows and true
meaning reveals itself from within the fabric of linquistics. Just as it is possible to
get caught in narrow definitions and thus fail to communicate with words,
conversely, if one tracks the thread of the meaning of language to its origin, a greater
meaning sometimes unfolds.

Just as "a house divided against itself cannot stand," (Mark 3:25), a person lacking harmony with the soul feels miserable and has no true power. By the same token, when you experience attunement with the soul, your life will take on a peace, charm and purpose unimaginable to the average person. When you are in tune with the soul, you have returned home to your true self.

The soul is the God presence in our personal human reality. It is God energy coalesced into the atoms of human form; it is eternal and lives in constant, unbroken communion with the source. A human mother is related to her offspring as long as life goes on. Some of her children may move far away and not see her again, perhaps severing all contact with her, but she is still their mother and lives on in the very cells of their being. This human relatedness cannot be revoked just as the relatedness between God and human is an eternal reality. The only way to have separation from the God source is to imagine it in the limited, finite human mind and then pretend this imagined illusion is the reality. In a state of such spiritual estrangement, the creative power of the soul attracts situations and experiences that make it seem like you are alone and separate, but as soon as you see beyond this delusion, you will feel alone and separate no longer. You see beyond it when you transcend the limited boundaries of your own mind and feel the soul. Only then can you feel the joy, bliss, peace and power that is the soul's nature.

The first experience of this state of consciousness is always a surprise to the finite, conscious mind because it does not have the capacity even to imagine such a state. But along with that surprise is a relief that is nearly overwhelming, for each human being recognizes this bliss and knows that he has returned to his true home.

When seen visibly, this divine essence appears as shimmering light, a dance of energy atoms. When felt emotionally, it is blissful ecstasy, utter unconditional love. When experienced intuitively, it is wisdom direct from the source, perfect knowingness beyond logic, what is sometimes referred to as gnosis.

One taste of this state of consciousness is more deeply satisfying than any awareness that the mind can produce, more pleasurable than any physical experience, more blissful than any emotion. Many people have this first taste of home during a rebirthing session. One man began weeping for joy and loudly cried out, "This is better than any drug! I have been looking everywhere for this and it was inside me all along!" Every individual is seeking the actual, direct connection with this blissful divine love of the soul and nothing less than this ultimate experience will satisfy.

Your true identity is the soul. Before your body began to come into existence, you as the soul were floating in space, blissfully peaceful and fully identified as part of God. No lack, no need and no anxiety impinged on this perfect state. Like an actor puts on a costume and a pretended identity to play a role on stage, you clothed your true self with the apparel of a physical body and formed attributes of conscious mind and personality. Then, forgetting that it was a costume you were wearing, that the personality was a pretended identity and not even remembering that you were on a stage, you also forgot your purpose for coming onto this stage in the first place.

When a woman impersonates a man, she does not become a man. When the almighty soul masquerades as either a man or a woman, it becomes neither but retains all the power of its divine nature regardless of whether or not the conscious mind or personality of an individual is aware of it. A human being reincarnates on earth over and over again until such time as he consciously regains his true status as a divine child of God. When, finally, he begins to attune with the soul, his ordinary self-conscious life gradually merges into the higher way of superconscious life. The soul begins to clear away blockages to health, intimacy, natural playfulness and authenticity. Once the soul takes up conscious residence in the body and mind, it directs and creates life with a magnificent purpose, clarity and power the rational mind, alone, could never even imagine.

Most people on earth today are unaware of these truths. They have moved away from home, from conscious contact with the soul. As long as a human being remains asleep to the truth of his identity, his abandoned soul is sentenced to remain in exile, imprisoned without contact with his awareness. Here there is no chance for real peace, for the soul is ever waiting for reunion and will not go unheard. Free will is never taken away, so each human being is consciously reunited with his soul only when he so chooses. Because the happiness he is seeking can be found only in the love of the soul, the pain of separation grows more and more intense, until he is willing to allow conscious reconnection with the soul. The pain, then, is sometimes the soul's way of coaxing him along to surrender to this reunion.

> To help us come back home,
> God sends many teachers.
> If we do not listen,
> He sends the great teacher - *Suffering* -
> *and then we listen.*

Unfortunately, we often do not begin to surrender to the reunion with the soul until God gets our attention through suffering. The painful circumstances around the earth today may be related to the tremendous energy which is stirring within the human family. A great awakening is at hand and the call has gone out to a multitude of individuals to begin to listen. As a planetary race, it is time to release our limited, time-bound conceptions in order to perceive our true spiritual identity.

3

A Time for Awakening

Awake, little one, and prepare to arise
Feel My life force stirring within
Awaken and wash the sleep from your eyes
For your life is about to begin.

You have lain dormant for thousands of years
Precious seed planted safe in earth's bed
I have nurtured and watered you with My tears
Come and dance in the magic ahead.

You have long dreamed of threat and harm
Nightmares that seemed so real.
So I wrapped My Light 'round your growing form,
Held you tight through your dream ordeal.

And I've kept your seat ever safe for you
Never again, little one, will you roam
For your time in the shroud is finally through
Arise, take my hand and come home.
                              Christina Thomas

   The Industrial Age has ended and the world has come fully
into the Information Age. There is now so much information
that even with the fastest computers, it is difficult to keep up.
Along with this tremendous expansion, it seems, simultaneously, that the world is shrinking. Everyday we watch as
events occurring on the other side of our planetary home
appear live on the television screens in our living rooms and
we begin to feel more akin to one another than in times past.
In July 1989, millions of us in the Western Hemisphere
watched as Chinese students in Tiananmen Square marched

for freedom carrying placards written in English, and felt that those young students could be our own children. More recently, we watched and some of us wept for joy as our brothers and sisters in Moscow stood steadfast and, at risk of their lives, refused to be dominated by Communism any longer. Our world is becoming smaller, more familiar, less disconnected, more homogenous.

UNDERSTANDING HUMAN LIFE

While we know a lot about a lot of things, most of us know very little about the workings of ourselves. What really makes a human being "tick" emotionally, psychologically and spiritually?

I frequently find that people are truly eager to have such information about themselves for it supplies answers to questions they did not know how to formulate but which are of such vital interest that an excitement begins to build at just the mention of the subject. There is little wonder that we feel excited for there is much to discover as we explore inner space. It could be said that human beings are equipped with a magnificent circuitry that is capable of feats so remarkable the conscious mind has difficulty comprehending them. A growing number of people are living the superconscious experiences of which the human instrument is capable.

A QUANTUM LEAP IS IMMINENT

Most people have not even glimpsed what is upon us, just as eons ago, creatures which had always lived in the ocean could not have known that other animals would leave the sea to live on dry land. When the time came, however, those creatures which were biologically ready responded to an instinctive call to make that quantum leap. Similarly, mankind today is standing on the very brink of a quantum leap in consciousness and individuals who have evolved sufficiently are responding to the great awakening which is upon us.

We know that human life begins at conception with the fertilization of a single cell, which divides itself into two cells, then four, then eight, then multiplies exponentially as the human baby body is formed. This can be compared to very simple, one-celled amoebic forms of life evolving into higher and more complex forms. During its formation, the human embryo continues its retracing of ancient life patterns, briefly looking much like a tadpole, then a fish, then successively higher forms of life.

All life forms which are lower than human life participate in a group consciousness. Individual animals share in the group soul energy which enlivens the species. This group energy defines, through the compulsion of instinct, how that animal group will function, what their nature and behavioral traits will be, how and what they will eat, how and when they will procreate, how they will parent their offspring and every other aspect of their existence. Creatures at this level have no free will and cannot decide any feature of life, nor even think about life, but are bound by natural law to function according to instinct. Animals have simple consciousness - they are aware of things around them - but are not aware that they are aware. Another way to say this is that no animal has self consciousness.

When the first human incarnation is reached, the individual soul or God essence enters.* Language is possible and this creature, now no longer merely animal but human, is self conscious — he is aware of himself and aware that he is aware. He has the latent ability to think and use his free will for good or ill. He also now has an inborn conscience and, with it, a sense of sin. The human often thinks that he is his body and also frequently identifies himself as being limited to his conscious mind and personality. When with sufficient evolution, he begins to realize that he is, primarily, the essence which fills the body, mind and personality, he feels less separate from others.

---

*A better comprehension of this dynamic could heal misunderstanding between the Darwinian evolutionists and the creationists for it was only the physical form of an animal which was utilized when the Creator intervened to implant the divine spark which is the soul. ("And He breathed into his nostrils the breath of life, and man became a living soul." Genesis 2:7). This intervention resulted in a quantum leap in consciousness for the newly-created species which was humankind. It was, then, not merely a natural evolutionary progression of ape becoming man. No ape species, through natural progression, would ever evolve into human. The implanting of the almighty soul in this new human creature set the species apart from all others. Of all creatures on earth, only the human possesses the unique, sensitive cerebro-spinal centers (chakras) which enable him, alone, to evolve to a full experience of divinity. With this awareness, it becomes clear that the theories of both the Darwinian evolutionists and the creationists are partially correct, although each lacks a vital element, for the human physical body did evolve from ape and divine intervention to create the new species did occur.

UNDERSTANDING DISCONTENT

As a small child, a human being is usually happy. If there is a sufficiently healthy, loving relationship with even one parent or parent-figure and adequate food, shelter and clothing, most human beings are happy during childhood. At puberty, however, something seems to go haywire and the same person becomes discontented and begins searching for something else, usually not knowing what that something is.

A birth supply of God energy seems to run out around puberty, at which time the individual may begin searching to find his own connection. This is the real idea behind puberty rites celebrated by so many cultures. Originally these rituals were to acknowledge that the young person was shifting from childhood dependence to more adult independence. Prior to puberty in such cultures, a youngster would be guided by parents and the family group. After puberty, he would be expected to begin individuating his feelings and values for himself. If he does experience this individuation process, the values he retains will acquire distinct, individual meaning for him and will not be merely an emulation or unquestioned acceptance of his parent or family. But regardless of cultural observance at puberty, if the young individual does not begin to make his own, authentic connection to the God energy at this point, he will not easily be able to step into the role of young adult, but will become increasingly unhappy. This discontent (which can be seen almost everywhere in our culture) is not accidental but is a natural element of self-conscious life and seems to be inherent in all human beings.

WHAT IS MISSING?

In case you are wondering what fiend would create a world where its hapless creatures are doomed to be unhappy, please continue reading, for there is a brighter side. It is precisely this discontent which is meant to signal the maturing individual that something is now missing. This haunting lack is meant to prod him to search and discover his true identity as a spiritual being. Like an automobile which begins to malfunction because some necessary lubricant has been used up, after puberty a person begins to feel that he is missing some essential element which was there before. A young person who experiences some disillusionment around puberty often carries the awareness of this lack quite consciously and frequently searches for life's meaning more passionately than others. Such a pubescent experience may manifest inwardly as in a dream, vision or direct intuition or it may be triggered by an outward event. In either case it becomes a wound that only the salve of the soul's love will heal. The only way any human being is going to experience any true, lasting happiness, whether at puberty or later in life, is through making this reconnection.

The whole process of seeking for that something which will satisfy the nagging spiritual deprivation could be compared to a person feeling extremely hungry and going out in search of food. He finds some vegetables laying on the ground and stops to pick them up. With ravenous appetite, he bites off several chunks and gulps them down, barely tasting. Only then does he realize, with a slightly sickening revulsion, that the vegetable had already begun to rot. He casts it away but is still hungry and that hunger keeps prodding him along in search of better nourishment. This happens repeatedly and he makes many distinctions about what qualities to look for in food. Eventually, he arrives at a beautiful, lush garden where the fruits and vegetables are nourishing and wholesome and the water life-giving.

In similar fashion, we try one experience after another in the desperate hope that we can find something that will satisfy the nagging hunger inside. It is not unusual to look outside for the soothing relief we seek. When we finally experience even a taste of the accepting, unconditional love of the soul, we realize, often for the first time, that this unrelenting inner lack is a spiritual hunger.

As miserable as self-conscious life can be, it is the necessary step between simple consciousness (animal life) and super-consciousness (God life). Through the learning and natural growth inherent in a person's life from pre-school through college years, a child matures into a fully-functioning member of society. In similar fashion, the many incarnations lived out on the plane of self-consciousness move the individual along an upwardly evolving path from barely awake (first stages of self-consciousness) to fully awake as a God-Being (super-consciousness).

TRANSFORMATION INTO GOD-LIFE

When a caterpillar becomes a butterfly, it weaves its cocoon out of material from its own body. After the caterpillar is encased in the cocoon, it is never possible for it to return to the old life. It must transform into the butterfly or die. The caterpillar is embodied in the beingness of the butterfly, however, just as the human child is embodied in the adult. It does not die in order to become a butterfly but must experience the process of metamorphosis, and the human child does not die in order to become an adult, but must grow and mature. In the same way, the merely self-conscious person must evolve over many lifetimes to transform into a superconscious being.

As any individual evolves into a higher being, he retains all the consciousness of the lower. Animals have simple consciousness only; human beings have simple consciousness (they are aware) and have self consciousness (they are aware that they are aware). As a human being gradually evolves to the first level of superconsciousness, he retains simple consciousness and self consciousness, and now gains superconsciousness.

The dawning of superconsciousness relates far more to energy field preparedness than to any mindset. While it is true that individuals nearing this advanced natural stage of evolution usually exhibit a very high moral character and generally have exceptionally high intelligence, this state is not a result of these qualities nor is the presence of these characteristics, alone, evidence of this level.

Superconsciousness cannot be earned by membership in any church or religion, nor is it awarded based on merit points accumulated for good works. It is not a result of measuring up to what society deems fit for a good person, nor is it forestalled by traits which society and culture judge as unacceptable. It is a sense (by whatever name it may be called) which gradually begins to dawn in that person who has reached a state of sufficient expansion over many lifetimes. Like the rising sun in the East begins to warm the landscape and burn away any fog in the atmosphere, a new clarity is born in the individual as the fog of self-conscious life evaporates in the morning sun of superconsciousness.

SUPERCONSCIOUSNESS - A UNIVERSAL EXPERIENCE

In the western world, the first broad stage of superconsciousness is often called Christ Consciousness. Because the word "Christ" is so generally associated with specific religious groups whose dogma excludes non-members, it is vitally important to understand that "Christ" Consciousness is neither the exclusive domain of nor is it limited in any way to any religion or culture. For the purposes of this book, when we say "Christ" Consciousness, the attempt is to describe that expanded state which is beyond the level of self-consciousness and which is a natural result of sufficient spiritual development in all evolving human beings. Other cultures use different names for this level of awareness.

The man, Jesus, born in Bethlehem of Jewish parents, had evolved over repeated lifetimes of spiritual work and purification to a place of superconsciousness. He fully lived sacred teachings which at that time were being intellectualized only. Jesus did not come to start a new religion and while it is true that a lot of people since then, including many

misguided ones, have started and practiced numerous the-
ologies borrowing His name, this in no way limits who He
was or the nature of his consciousness. If a person from your
town went to another region and began a business under
your name, the people in that vicinity might think that they
knew something about you because of that business. Would
that, however, really mean anything at all about you?
Wouldn't they have to meet you, personally, to actually
know you? More clarity around these often confusing and
emotionally-charged issues is vital. Freeing your mind of
some of the fears surrounding this subject will make it easier
to surrender to your own transformation into higher consciousness. The teachings of Jesus are as simple as they are
powerful. The gist of His message is: (1) Love (2) Don't judge.
The sincere practice of these teachings, alone, could heal the
whole world.

The presence of Jesus in physical form was two-fold: His
body was physical and human but the consciousness which
filled Him was entirely, completely superconsciousness, the
fog of self-consciousness having been burned away.

Jesus came to serve a great public mission as the first person
in our current cycle of world history who was filled with
superconsciousness. A primary element in His work was to
stimulate others to begin awakening their own potential as
superconsciousness beings. The life of Jesus was a great
signal that many human beings would eventually evolve
sufficiently to reach the advanced state. Never did Jesus
indicate that he, as a person, was the sole being who could
reach this place. On the contrary, his message was exactly the

opposite of this and His life was a model for sincere disciples to follow.*

When an individual reaches the first levels of superconsciousness, he will begin to experience changes, usually gradual, in his conscious awareness. First of all, he becomes more aware of his feelings, with a deeper level of compassion. He begins to experience true intimacy, allowing himself to be vulnerable and undefended with another person. Eventually he is able to feel a love for all creatures. Unconditional love is the hallmark of superconsciousness.

The individual is slowly expanding beyond the personal to become more transpersonal. He is becoming greater through continually expanding the limited boundaries of the lesser. The subtle cerebro-spinal centers evolve, with the growing capacity to pull in more and more energy from the universal energy field. He realizes that his real self is not limited to hs separate body, personality and emotions but is actually energy — the same energy which moves through other people.

*He prayed to God the Father that those awakened individuals would "...be one as we are" (St. John 17:11), God the Father being Cosmic Consciousness, the second great stage of superconsciousness. The consciousness of Jesus was one with Cosmic Consiousness and He was praying for others to experience this same union in consciousness. When Jesus said, "No man cometh to the Father except by me," (John 14:6), He was saying that no man could reach Cosmic Consciousness except by going through Christ Consciousness. (See chart entitled "Stages of Consciousness.") When He said, "...glorify thy Son..." (St. John 17:1), "Son" meant the consciousness which filled Him and which would fill and enliven any human able to evolve to a sufficiently advanced stage. The very essence of these words is impersonality; in no way was Jesus asking to have his ego glorified. As a matter of fact, Jesus' ego, having been completely purified of dross, was the very minimal necessary to keep His consciousness linked to the physical body.

After his own experience of spontaneous enlightenment in the late 19th century, Dr. Richard Maurice Bucke investigated this phenomenon of spiritual awakening extensively. He researched many suspected cases involving individuals who had lived in earlier centuries, and also interviewed a number of contemporaries, either personally or by mail, to elicit first-hand information about their experiences. He wrote of his findings in Cosmic Consciousness, which was first published in 1901. Like a trickle through a tiny hole in a dike presages a mighty breakthrough of waters rushing back home to the sea, Dr. Bucke believed that the cases of spiritual awakening which he documented were the forerunners of a new race of superconscious beings who would be born from among us in far greater numbers at some future time. More than nine decades have elapsed since the publication of that book, and much current evidence indicates that this long-awaited great awakening is now imminent. Humankind is pregnant with higher potential and a new consciousness is due. Mother earth's contractions grow more intense and the labor process seems well under way. The midwives are ready.

UNIVERSAL ENERGY FIELD

THE PROCESS OF AWAKENING

Ego — True Self

THE SOUND-ASLEEP GOD

● Ego is in the driver's seat. It runs the life from a defensive conviction that it is separate and alone. This big, inflated Ego consistently blocks out the light, love, power and creative genius available from the Universal Energy Field. Fear, guilt, scarcity and inadequacy dominate the life experience.

● Isolated by the prison of Ego limitations, this person acts from compulsive reaction and has little sense of power or choice in his life. The True Self is asleep.

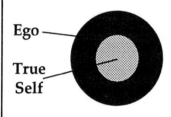

Ego — True Self

THE STIRRINGS OF DIVINITY

● Ego values still predominate but a persistent haunting discomfort and dissatisfaction begins to surface. Old Ego values, usually materialistic and pleasure-seeking, no longer suffice and a restless search begins for that "something else" which will bring true meaning to the life.

● Occasional glimpses of the joy of the True Self begin to encourage the person along his journey and leave him ever more dissatisfied with the emptiness of a life which lacks the spiritual dimension. This person is less compulsive, less reactive and a little more free.

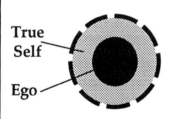

True Self — Ego

THE GOD IS AWAKENING

● The True Self is expanding. A greater sense of wholeness, connection and openness allows for more safety, love, free choice and a recognition of a higher life purpose. This person is happier because he is less self-conscious.

● The Ego, still shrinking and increasingly aligned with the Soul, blocks less light, love, power and creative genius - and is beginning to take its rightful place as the obedient servant of the Soul.

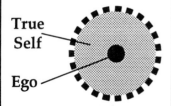

True Self — Ego

THE GOD IS AWAKENED

● The True Self is more fully expanded. This person is autonomous and realizes his true identity as the Soul. Love, trust, abundance and oneness are his reality. Light, power and creative genius from the Universal Energy Field continuously infuse the True Self. This person feels love because he is in touch with its source within.

● Ego is now deflated, small and strong. Like a ballbearing, it serves the Soul's purpose by facilitating movement of the True Self in the physical world.

Notes

Notes

STAGES OF CONSCIOUSNESS

ANIMAL LIFE

SIMPLE
CONSCIOUSNESS

Group Consciousness
Aware of Surroundings
Survival Instinct
No Free Will

Lower
Receptual

Higher
Perceptual

Language Ability

Soul (God Essence) Enters

HUMAN LIFE

SELF
CONSCIOUSNESS

Aware That He is Aware
Conceptual Ability - Thinking
Free Will - Sense of Sin
Guilt - Separation

Inherent Discontent
Haunted by Unconscious
"Call of the Divine"
Senses Savior which is coming:
"CHRIST CONSCIOUSNESS'

The World of Maya (Duality)

"THE BIG MOVIE"
1 million (disease-free!) years
of normal, natural living required
to evolve from first human incarnation
to first stage of Super Consciousness

Sense of Separateness begins to dissolve. Telepathy becomes a generalized ability.

Aware that a human is a Divine Soul residing in a physical body.

GOD LIFE

SUPER
CONSCIOUSNESS

Aware Through Intuition
Continual Infusion of Life
from Within

1st Stage:
CHRIST
CONSCIOUSNESS

Aware of all, of others
Feels with all,
sorrow and joy
True Intimacy

2nd Stage:
COSMIC
CONSCIOUSNESS

Aware of Whole Cosmos
Beyond Creation
and Duality
Divine Detachment

A multitude of individuals are here ▲ ready to awaken into Christ Consciousness.

4

Becoming More Conscious

*Your sojourns in bodily form over repeated lifetimes
comprise a long round-trip journey, which culminates in
your conscious reunion with your soul. When, by gradually
becoming more conscious, you finally realize the truth of
your essential identity as a God-being, your life experience
will become filled with joy and you will be freed from the
necessity to reincarnate as a limited human being.*
Christina Thomas

There is a plethora of information available in the world
today, yet with all that is known about so many subjects,
most people know very little about the way their own consciousness works. Even though it is this element which
distinguishes a human being from all the other creatures on
earth, still it is practically the last subject to be studied. What
could possibly be more important than understanding yourself and discovering ways to be happier?

As you grow in awareness, it is helpful to learn how to
work more effectively with your own mind and personality.
Real-life examples can light the way as you build a bridge
from the old static mode of living to a more alive participa-
tion and conscious interaction in each moment of your life.
The new way of life is very different from the old. People who
experience this transformation are thrilled to discover that
they have arrived in a wonderful new land, but soon realize
that they are in need of guidance, for this new territory is
uncharted.

The new uncharted land is the inner territory of your own being. The information in this section will provide some practical guidelines for understanding and managing your own awareness process so that you can effectively integrate transformational experiences into a greater psychological and spiritual wholeness. If and when you find yourself in the throes of differentiating your own values and becoming your own person, this information will help in very practical ways.

NAVIGATING EGO'S MINEFIELD

Many people are completely dominated by ego and approach life almost exclusively from a self-centered orientation. This is not even questioned, for few people have any understanding that there are happier alternatives. To live less selfishly actually feels like death to the ego. This feeling of dying is the ego's fear, for it knows that true, unconditional love is a threat to its power.

The little, separate ego mind is like a sugar cube in the hand of a person standing on a diving board. If the sugar cube had awareness, it might be saying, "Oh! If I don't get him out of here, this will finish me off! If he dives into that water, it will be the end of me!"

The water is the pure love of the soul. The ego fears love most of all for it knows it cannot maintain its selfish, controlling domination of the mind and personality in the presence of love. Though ego is not completely eliminated by the process, it does dissolve somewhat so that, like the sugar cube, its boundaries are not the same as before. Imagine the utter futility: what you want most of all in your life is love, and ego wants most of all to keep you from experiencing real love. Many times you will think you are actually going to reach the object of your desire but when you near it, something occurs to keep love away from you. The ego plays this game over and over again in one real-life drama after another, keeping you in bondage like a hostage held prisoner by a brain-washing terrorist, a terrorist who is literally incapable of love and who has no understanding of what love is in the first place.

Ego fights very hard to keep its control over your life, waging its battle in many different and confusing ways. One of ego's very effective tactics is to erode your confidence and energy by use of a negative inner voice. The chart entitled "Soul and Ego Qualities" (at the end of this chapter), can help you find balance as you go about the work of differentiating your own innermost feelings and voices. Ego's negative voice attempts to divert you from true love and is often a merciless and unrelenting companion. Though you will not be able to completely silence it, you can become very skillful at responding to your own ego in a way which empowers you. I have included here some examples of actual dialogue with the negative voice of ego, which can be helpful as models in similar situations.

As I reached a supermarket, I began to feel the tremendous love which accompanies a spontaneous expansion of the heart center. A few minutes later, inside the store, I passed an old couple pushing a grocery cart and felt the most exquisite love for them, almost unbearable in its intensity. Moving silently past them, I went on through the store, gathering the items on my grocery list, all the while enveloped in the nearly overwhelming force of love surging through me. (Even mundane activities like grocery shopping take on a magical quality when love is present!) Then a thought came into my mind, the negative voice of ego, saying, "You must be crazy to feel like this with all the problems in your life!" (There were some difficult circumstances in my life at that time.)

My response to ego was: "You may be right. Maybe I am crazy, but I am going to feel this anyway. If I am a fool, then I am a loving fool!" The negative chatter stopped abruptly.

The ego mind wants you to think about your troubles. It wants you to pay attention to everything that is wrong. If it can keep you busy with a focus on problems and fears, it can keep you distracted from *its* greatest fear - the love which awaits when you contact the soul. So when you turn your attention to things of beauty and pure love, ego usually becomes very agitated. It wants to change the subject and get you away from those beautiful thoughts and feelings because to allow them to continue is for the ego to risk dissolution. (The sugar cube wants to get you away from the threat of water.)

Another time the negative ego attempted to sieze control as I arrived at a dinner party. Just as I entered a room full of dinner guests, the following thought came into my mind: "There's Jack. How arrogant he is!"

My inward response to my ego was, "I don't feel that way. That isn't my thought. This is you, always judging everybody, and it makes me miserable when you do this. Is this what you're going to do all evening? Well, I'm not going to go along with it. I may not be able to stop you from doing this but every time you do it, I am going to go directly to that person and give him as much love as I can." The inner, critical voice ceased its judging for the rest of that evening.

It may be helpful here to have some clarification of "giving as much love as I can." This does not mean that I would say even one word about my inner experience to the person. After all, it is not *his* problem that my ego is noisily chattering in my head. And the judgment by my petty little ego that Jack is arrogant means nothing about Jack. On the contrary, it says a lot about the arrogance of the ego itself.*

Another very common trait of negative ego manifests itself in the desire to be right. This stems from ego's fear that it must prove itself repeatedly by competing. Most people do not realize that they would rather be right than happy and ego has no difficulty in running rough-shod over their most precious relationships. The desire of ego to be right shows

---

*A tactical trick of ego is to point out faults in others that actually are faults of itself. Thus ego creates confusion and keeps a person from working on his own faults. An appropriate way to love Jack in this situation might be just a pleasant, sincere greeting or, depending on the relationship, a warm hug. Or it might involve no direct exchange with Jack at all but only my inward visualization of him surrounded in love and light, feeling peaceful, happy and having a good time. Under all circumstances, it would always involve common sense and propriety.

itself in a thousand ways in everyday life, and it is extremely helpful to have practical tools to begin to combat its onslaught. One need not look far to find an example. I will use an experience that occurred when I was in the process of writing my first book, Secrets.

First of all, my inner direction to write that book was very clear and I felt focused and inspired to keep moving it toward completion. I told a few friends and family members that I was writing a book, but (as I realized later) they really did not take me seriously and I was very much alone with the project.

Ego relentlessly berated me, "This is irresponsible, taking all this time to write. Nobody is going to read this book; you have nothing to say that has not already been said. This book is not needed. You will find that it will be a big failure and then you will have wasted all this time." I felt vulnerable and knew that the negative rantings and ravings of this unwelcome inner critic might well be true. I dealt with it by agreeing.

"You may be right," I would respond to the attacks. "This book may be the biggest flop that has ever been written; perhaps not even one person will read it. And I will then have to accept that it is a total failure and that I wasted all this time and spent money for a word processor needlessly. But I feel I must write it anyway. If I find I have made a mistake, I am willing to forgive myself and go on with my life, but I would feel too uncomfortable if I refused to follow the strong inner promptings which I feel are urging me to write."

Because I did not resist these negative fears but actually surrendered to the possibility that these results could happen, ego could not disempower me. The ego is addicted to being right and I was placating it by giving it some of the substance to which it is addicted. It would then keep somewhat more quiet while I went on writing. It was, of course, very important for me to be certain that I actually was willing to face these possible negative consequences.

A happy footnote to the whole experience is the tremendously positive effect Secrets has had in my life and in the lives of others. Many people have contacted me to tell me of the benefit they have experienced because of it. If I had not found a way to keep writing during the barrage of inner doubts, this benefit would have been missed. Because I kept following my heart and moving toward my goal, my life and the lives of many other people are richer.

Your spirit is never afraid; only ego is capable of fear. It is well worth learning to use this or some other process to deal effectively with any fear which arises to keep you stuck in a stagnant status quo or otherwise threatens to squelch your spirit when you are longing to live your dream.

LET THE SOUL LEAD

The soul is perfect wisdom and balance. Unlike the separate, ego mind, the soul's response is always perfect appropriateness. When you rely only on the logic and understanding of your conscious mind, you are limited indeed. It is no wonder that many people are afraid to make decisions. If you think that your conscious (ego) mind is the authority and power in your life, you have every reason to be fearful. The ego mind attempts to arrive at conclusions based on logic and the dialectics of either inductive or deductive reasoning, all of which often result in false conclusions. But the soul can see around corners and when you begin to tune into its wisdom, you are allowing a higher, natural perfection to bring a beautiful order to your life.

This requires your willingness to confront your own ego over and over again, which can seem like a ceaseless task, especially in the beginning. Later you will see wonderful results from your efforts and will, naturally, be encouraged to continue. This process is one of differentiating your own inner feelings and inner voices as you gradually peel yourself away from total identity with the little separate ego and begin to realign with the soul. The chart entitled "The Process of Awakening," can serve you in this effort.

This process of differentiating your own values reminds me of the tuning of a fine piano. The piano tuner strikes the tuning fork, listens to its perfect tone, and plays a note on the piano. The note is off-key. He tightens the string inside the piano which corresponds to that key, repeatedly sounds the tone on the tuning fork, and listens with sensitive, trained ears until the tightening action brings that note into perfect pitch. He continues this process until the entire keyboard is perfectly in tune.

How helpful it would be to remember this metaphor when your own strings are being 'tightened' in order to bring the instrument of your being into perfect attunement with the soul. The tone is perfect for the individual note and, in addition, it is perfect in its relationship to both neighboring and distant keys. The entire keyboard, each note individually attuned to itself and its immediate group, synchronizes to form one precision instrument that plays in harmony. This could describe a person living his own individual life powerfully and successfully, then, being in attunement with his own soul, relating to others in his family and neighborhood in a supportive way. Such a harmonious grouping would interact peacefully and brilliantly with the distant notes of other synchronous groupings of people around our planet, able to harmonize all activities for the highest good of all.

Peace for all begins with peace in the individual. A person who has turmoil within can never link with another to create harmony. Such a person usually lacks peace even in a primary personal relationship like marriage. Only as each individual comes into attunement with the overlighting spirit of his soul can he come into balance with another individual. Two or three attuned individuals living and relating harmoniously with each other form a powerful unit for creating more of the same.

EGO'S TRUE PURPOSE

With all the comments about the negative aspects of ego, it may be helpful to discuss its positive functions. The ego's true purpose is to protect the physical body as the vehicle and residence of the indwelling soul. It is a protective friend when it keeps you from real physical danger, but over many centuries of interaction within the cellular life of the human race, it has gotten out of hand. Ego tends to be an alarmist. Too often, it goes way overboard and stimulates fear, guilt, judgment and other negative, destructive feelings when there is no real danger. It is meant to work like an instrument in a cockpit giving accurate readings. An altimeter's function, for example, is to indicate how high the plane is flying. It is not necessary or appropriate for it to decide anything, nor to fly the plane. All that is needed from that device is an accurate indication of the altitude, but if that instrument goes overboard the way ego often does, even if the plane is flying at an appropriate, safe altitude, the meter might begin flashing: "Danger! Danger! Pull out! Crash imminent!" In reality, there may be no danger at all. In most cases, the ego must be re-trained to perform its appropriate work and no more.

Another metaphor may contribute to greater understanding. Ego is like a man who is qualified only to be a butler at the royal palace, but at a moment when no one is looking, he sneaks into the throne room and pretends to be the King. In order to maintain this farce, he lies and makes up stories and generally manipulates everything and everyone, with an interest only in protecting his own base of power. Because he has dressed himself in the King's regal attire and is seated on the throne, his "act" can be very confusing, indeed. When he makes a decision which turns out to be wrong, he will blame it on someone else. The people whose jobs and lives are at his mercy will feel very insecure and will run scared. The role of a worthy King is to serve his people, but this despot's rulership will be a reign of terror. He will retain his lofty seat, however, until it is realized that he is an imposter. Once this occurs, he must be removed from the throne, be made to obey his superiors and discipline himself to responsibly perform only the duties of his own job. He must be made to keep quiet when serious affairs of state are discussed, for all he is actually qualified to do is open the door when a guest arrives.

The ego's real job is to be the obedient servant of the soul. The soul, alone, is fit to be the King on the throne of your life. When the servant is needed, he can effectively serve only if he is well trained. When you go into the world to achieve a task, you can then rely on the discipline of this servant to do his job well. For instance, during the process of writing this book, it is inspiration from the soul which stimulates the ideas in my mind, but a well-trained, obedient ego servant is needed in order to submit to the long hours it takes to get all the inspirational ideas onto paper in an organized, intelligible fashion. While a recalcitrant ego would create frequent distractions ("let's stop writing and go eat something!"), a well-disciplined ego will cooperate.

THE EGO MUST BE TRAINED

I have found that it can be effective to interact with the ego in somewhat the same way one would deal with a pet — a big dog, for instance -- firmly and clearly showing him what is expected. If the animal obeys well, I would pat him and treat him affectionately. When my ego servant is supporting a

project, like working for long hours on this book, I often will
find some very positive way to reward that part of myself. I
might, for instance, have a massage or take a long, relaxing
bath or purchase some perfume or item of clothing that
makes me feel like smiling. Then the ego is willing to continue its cooperation and support without sabotaging worthy projects.

Recently I observed a beautiful seeing-eye dog with its
master. It occurred to me that the ego could be compared to
that animal. In the department store, when the blind person
stopped to chat with someone, the big dog sat calmly by his
side. There was such synchrony between them, and the dog
had such an aura of dignity, dedication and purpose that it
brought tears to my eyes. I watched them nearly awestruck.
A harmonious energy emanated from the pair, as the blind
man went about his business without any special attention to
the dog, appearing to take the dog's service for granted.
"This is what a well-trained, disciplined ego is like," I thought.
"It is very strong and alert and serves its master with complete submission, without demanding attention for itself.
Performing its job well, it also gets treated very well — better
than it would be treated in any other circumstance. As a
matter of fact, a seeing-eye dog is allowed entrance to places
where no other animal would be admitted. Because of the
selfless service he performs, such a dog is treated like he is
more than a dog." As the analogy continued to play itself out
in my mind, I went on with my shopping, feeling that the
seeing-eye dog had been a great teacher for me that day.

EGO STRENGTH IS NEEDED

Without going too deeply into the subject of ego formation, it is important to recognize that ego plays an important and appropriate role in human life. Each baby is born afresh, carrying with it the energy records of its past lives. The ego structure in each incarnation is built by utilizing as scaffolding the constructs of belief systems, religious precepts and cultural values learned from family, religion and society. These values, which are acquired without question on the part of the child, are undifferentiated. They are not really his values for he has not examined them to determine whether or not they are true for him. If he does go about the process of differentiation at some point in life, whatever values he retains or adopts will then become his authentic values, for he will have chosen them consciously. When a person has done this work of differentiation, his life becomes more integrated and whole and is a conduit for the powerful energy of the soul. If another person performs the very same activity merely as a function of ego without undergoing this process, it may seem hollow because it lacks the authenticity of his own individual, conscious differentiation. It is not the value itself, which must be questioned then, but the energy or lack of energy behind the value.

For further understanding, let us continue to use the above analogy of erecting a building to represent the growth process of a life. For a laborer to work on the building itself, the scaffolding must be sufficiently stable; if the scaffolding wobbles too much, a workman will be so preoccupied with surviving a possible collapse of the platform on which he is standing that he will be unable to devote attention to making progress on the actual building. The scaffolding is a symbol for the ego structure. When this functions appropriately, providing reliable support, one is free to construct the building of his life with no need to be preoccupied with the condition of the scaffolding on which he stands.

A stable scaffolding correlates to a childhood in a sufficiently healthy family with adequately sound religious, social and cultural values.* No inordinately destructive threat impinges on the growing child's awareness and a strong, solid ego structure forms. In adulthood, when sufficient maturity is reached and the construct of the ego is strong enough, he can safely begin to dismantle the scaffolding. He then will be whole enough to begin examining his acquired values one by one and determine for himself from his own, unique, personal, inner feelings just what he really does or does not believe. He will be free of the need to pretend belief in a value in order to purchase the affection or approval of anyone else. Differentiating his own feelings and values thusly, he will discover his true life.

It can be detrimental to attempt the work of differentiation prematurely, for you cannot surrender what you do not own. Until the ego is sufficiently strong, you cannot transcend it. Be willing to bow to the timing of your soul, for it knows best what you are ready for. A caterpillar emerges from its cocoon only when the butterfly is ready to fly. Practice letting it be

*See Chart entitled "Stages of Faith"

okay that the formation of your life takes whatever time it does. An exercise to help you practice this is included in the chapter entitled "Attitudes of Attunement."

When you are ready to begin the process of differentiation, you must examine each value as it presents itself in your life. You must honestly observe each construct and decide what meaning it has for you. At this point, either (a) you will take on the task of peeling away the defenses, illusions, and pretenses of your own ego (a process which, though painful, will eventually liberate you), or (b) you will refuse to claim ownership of these energy structures (for example, fear, guilt, self-righteousness, anger, resentment, judgment) and will then project them outward onto other people and other things. You will not only never become free through this approach, but will also become less and less happy.

Please understand that it is not appropriate and not possible to eliminate ego altogether. For as long as you occupy a physical body, you need its support, but ego makes a terrible master. It is desirable to train it so that it becomes the obedient servant of your soul. Only by taking up the challenge of confronting your own negative ego structures one by one will you ever begin to free yourself and bring the ego into obedient submission to serve the work your soul longs to do. When this is accomplished, you will feel a tremendous joy and sense of purpose in your life.

As a caterpillar does not die but surrenders its limited identity to become a butterfly, the greater Self is born only upon the surrender of the little egoistic self. Just as the caterpillar cannot possibly comprehend what life as a butterfly will be like, so the little egoistic self lacks the capacity to fathom the magnificence and expansion of the multi-dimensional life that awaits one who awakens to the love and wisdom of the soul.* When the caterpillar spins the cocoon out of its own body and the door closes behind, that chrysalis must seem like a tomb. When you reach a similar place in the natural process of transformation, it may feel the same way. This chrysalis stage is usually very inactive and most people have been well trained to value only activity and doingness. The greatest growth and progress that can be made during the chrysalis stage, however, occurs through yielding to beingness. The noblest form of activity during such a phase is to surrender to the higher intelligence, trusting that there is meaning to the process.

A sufficiently conscious person is willing to go through the daily process of sorting out his own authentic feelings in order to discover who he really is. To undergo this process, he will need ego strength. At the same time, he will need flexibility to surrender to Spirit's penetration and subsequently to gestate and birth the offspring of that creative union into consciousness. When a person touches the energy of the Soul, there is always a resulting creativity to be expressed. It may or may not be in the arts but it will always be unique and creative, for God never duplicates and each human being is as magnificently unique as fingerprints or snowflakes.

*"...he that loseth his life for my sake will find it."(Matthew 10:39). Here Jesus was speaking not of his personal human self when he said "my sake," but was referring to the presence of the Christ Consciousness, which he fully expressed and which filled him. This same impersonal spirit of superconsciousness is expressed by Paramahansa Yogananda as "When that i shall die, then shall I know who am I."

Soul and Ego Qualities

Ego Qualities	Soul Qualities
Fearful	Loving
Guilt (self-indulgent focus)	Corrects behavior & forgives self
Shame (self-judgment)	Joy! Inner work to feel the soul's love
Phony	Authentic
Feels separate, alone.	Feels unified with others.
Goals are based on fear, scarcity	Goals align with Soul Purpose
Critical of self and others	Accepts self and others
Takes self very seriously	Healthy sense of humor
Fragmented	Integrated - Has Integrity
Manipulative, cunning	Truthful
Full of pride, boastful, braggart	Peaceful. True humility
Rather be right than happy	Chooses love; learns from mistakes
Loses peace with changes	Happiness not based on circumstances
Blaming; wants others to change	Seeks results without blaming
Feels desperate, suspicious	Trusting
Confused - shifting priorities	Clear about priorities
Judgmental	Tolerant, accepting of self and others
Always comparing, competing	Honors uniqueness of self & others
Fearful of scarcity, deprivation	Feels abundant, safe
Acquisitive, greedy, jealous	Generous. Rejoices with others
Tense	Relaxed
Self-serving	Yearns to truly serve
Controlling of other people	In control of self & lets others be
Seeks to get love from outside	Feels love from within - content
Seeks escape from self-awareness	Introspection for greater awareness

When negative behavior or results signal that you have become caught in ego's territory, this chart can be utilized as a map to find your way back to the domain of the Soul. Using it as a tool to evaluate, compete, compare or judge yourself or another in any way will not serve the highest good.

Stages of Faith

Conception & Gestation. An incarnation begins at conception as the soul joins the first fertilized cell and begins directing cell division and the evolving formation of the embryo and fetus. The soul is omniscient - all knowing; this super level of awareness functions in the forming baby like a wide open psychic receptor. The baby knows at a deep cellular level what is *really* going on in his family. He feels one with his mother and absorbs the thoughts and *particularly* the feelings of his parents, especially mother. If unusually traumatic events occur during conception, gestation, labor, birth or right after birth (e.g., separation from mother/parents as happens with adoption), baby often will carry a deeply unconscious anxiety or outright fear that may result in his being timid or somewhat untrusting.

Birth and Infancy. This stage relates to the building of trust wherein mother is God. Mother is the first God an infant knows. She is all-powerful and holds his very survival in her hands. The experience with her tells him what God is like. If his parents wanted him and he is fed sufficiently, held, cuddled and touched enough, kept comfortably warm or cool, talked to . . . if he is generally made safe and nurtured adequately to meet his needs *according to his own inner "nurturometer,"* he quickly grows through the infantile stage. Mother has been there for him and he has learned that he can trust her presence and support. This translates within him to an unconscious trust that life is good and the world is a safe place to be. Absorbing enough of what he needs as an infant, he is sufficiently empowered to move to the next stage. When deprivation is too severe or experience too traumatic, some degree of neurosis results, which the growing child must deal with in some way.

	EMPOWERMENT	NEUROSIS
Early Childhood	Autonomy	Shame & Fear
School	Initiative	Guilt, Timidity
Pre-pubescent	Industry	Inferiority
Teen	Identity and role confusion. If we have learned to do something, we think we are something.	
Adult	Intimacy Productivity	Isolation Addictions
Mid-30s	Generative Creativity	Stagnation Boredom
Fifties and Beyond		
	Integrity	Despair

This chart lists the sequence of one incarnation and we have many, many lifetimes. Most lives are a blending of characteristics shown in the Empowerment and Neurosis columns. If there are deprivations, insufficiencies or other traumas in the gestation, birth or early childhood stages, some degree of neurosis usually results and becomes magnified as long as it remains unresolved. It is this broad area which is the current focus of human psychology. If your experience has been less ideal than that shown on the left, which is the experience of most people, all is not lost. Everything can be healed if you are willing to approach the work of healing with honesty.

Your own unique contribution
and creative expression is needed,
for the Universe never makes a mistake
and if you were not needed,
you would not be here.
To live in tune with the Soul
is your ultimate destiny,
the very purpose for which
you are in a human form.
Bringing the outer world and the
inner world into harmony
is essential in this process and to
the extent that you achieve this alignment,
to that extent will you be happy.

5

Dreams and Visions

*I will pour out my spirit upon all flesh; and your sons and
your daughters shall prophesy, your old men shall dream
dreams, your young men shall see visions.*
Joel 2:28, 29

In the western cultures, the functions of the conscious mind
and left-brained, logical thought have been given very high
value, while the intuitive, right-brained faculties have been
regarded as less significant. Medical science now recognizes
that health, happiness and general well-being suffer greatly
without the normal day-to-day right-brained functions. By
becoming more attuned to the soul, you may begin opening
to the more intuitive parts of yourself. Dreaming can be
especially important in this regard and serves very practical
and beneficial purposes.

Like the stars in the sky, which are always there but can
only be seen at night, it is suspected that human beings are
always dreaming, but are usually only *aware* of dreams which
occur during sleep. People are normally unaware of many of
their waking dreams because the conscious mind closes the
door from the unconscious, where dreams originate. Because of this, it is often easier to recall a dream which occurs
while the conscious mind is at rest. The only time the conscious mind of the average person is completely off duty is
during sleep, and then it is *only* the conscious mind which
sleeps.

The idea of daydreams is familiar to most people. Usually one thinks of them as fantasies which appear and play themselves out on what could be called an inner viewing screen in the mind. Daydreams occur when the dreamer is in an awake but relaxed state.

When you dream, you are experiencing the fourth dimension. *Three* dimensions refers to length, width and depth — factors whose constancy depends on a linear measurement of time. Time is the basic variable between the third and fourth dimensions. All dreams occur in the fourth-dimension, which is beyond time. Timelessness characterizes the fourth dimension and the dream state, and along with this variation, space also expands. We experience this in dreams when a person or event from the past coincides with a person or event from the present or future, all superimposed without the limitations of time or the parameters of space.

DREAMS SERVE PRACTICAL, VALUABLE PURPOSES

Sometimes both sleeping and waking dreams relieve a build-up of psychic and emotional tension, which the conscious mind has failed to acknowledge. In this way, dreams can serve as a vent or safety valve and help to maintain a stable intrapersonal equilibrium. At other times, they may help to reorient the dreamer when he is deviating from some important focus. Through the dream the unconscious may be saying, "Pay attention to this!" This kind of dream can provoke valuable reevaluation and adjustment, and serve as a form of inner guidance.

The more you honor your dreams and inner processes, the better they can begin to serve you. The mechanism which allows dreams to be remembered consciously becomes more responsive as you become accustomed to paying attention to dream messages. As a result, a more continuous flow of communication is allowed to become conscious, bringing with it whole new dimensions of awareness. Life takes on greater meaning and becomes more filled with deep feeling, intuitive insights and synchronistic happenings. Creative energy pours into the consciousness and a new sense of purpose is born. Being more open to and conversant with the unconscious is like having a brilliant, supportive friend in a back room who consistently gives you valuable, accurate information and trustworthy assistance. When you are the fortunate recipient of such invisible, right-brained knowing- ness, you can utilize the left-brained logical mind much better, too, and begin living even closer to the unconscious. Most dreams originate in the subconscious mind, although an occasional, unusually numinous dream may stem from the collective unconscious or even from the limitlessness of superconsciousness.

GLIMPSING THE FOURTH DIMENSION

Despite the awe or fear which sometimes surrounds them, visions are natural and occur more often than most people probably realize. These final years of the twentieth century are a time of great change, not only externally but especially in consciousness. A spiritual transformation, unlike any- thing in recorded history, has begun and is gathering momentum. Increasing numbers of individuals are awakening to expanded levels of the mind which have long lain dormant within. Mankind is perched right on the brink of an energetic shift into a higher state of being.

The opening of the heart center occurs when an individual reaches the first degrees of this aspect of superconscious life. There is an experience of unconditional love and the awareness that there is no essential separation one human being from another. Many people are in form right now whose role is to serve this awakening process throughout our planetary family. Sometimes this awakening is followed in the individual by an ecstatic vision. It is my hope that the information in this section will provide assistance and encouragement for better understanding and integration of such an experience.

I think of visions as being very numinous waking dreams. Always filled with divine energy and originating in the superconscious realms, they are harbingers of great change in the visionary's life. When I had my first vision in 1984 (as described in Secrets), I knew intuitively that my life would never be the same again. This has proven to be true. Although the new, spiritual energy took over somewhat gradually, that vision marked the moment when I became *consciously* aware that my soul was going to run the show in my life from then on.

Visions are actually very practical. Those which I have experienced all serve very vital functions which enhance everyday life in dynamic ways. Some explain how to redirect a facet of life in a significant manner, others provide clarification about some critical issue, and still others bring about deep healing and integration. I have even experienced visions that involve the welfare and healing of great numbers of people, sometimes with specific directions regarding how I am to proceed with playing my role in supporting them.

Information and awareness received in this way always hit home, communicating perfectly. Also, because the experience is fourth-dimensional and thus beyond time, that which occurs in a few seconds of clock time usually requires much longer to describe. When written, for instance, an inner event originally lasting only a few minutes might fill an entire book and still fall short of adequate description.

I have experienced visions when I was not aware of a specific non-physical presence but felt powerful numinous energy. Communication is sometimes verbal but more often is telepathic. Sometimes, although only a brief sentence is expressed in actual words, it will trigger the unfolding of whole meanings within the mind in an infusion of knowingness from within. In this way, part of the brain/mind is being stimulated to release a potency latent within it all along, much as a seed releases the flowering plant it always contained in potentiality.

When we merely recall a memory, we *mentally* move back to a time in the past. Time is a quality of third-dimensional reality, and fourth-dimensional experiences exist outside of time. Therefore, when remembered, they are often experienced all over again, rather than merely reiterated mentally. It is as though the person steps back into that portion of a universal hologram which contains the past event in an ever-present time-space continuum. Because of this perpetual present-time quality, it is easier to relate a fourth-dimensional occurrence in the present tense. As it is described, it is sometimes re-experienced by the visionary with all the vivid color, sound and feeling tone originally felt. At such times, listeners often receive their own powerful, life-changing shifts in awareness. Many of them may feel the strong, ecstatic energy which infuses the visionary, and some can actually see in internal vision what the visionary sees.

Visions are mystical, but they need not be mysterious. I will attempt to de-mystify this subject as I share personal experiences which have been healing, practical and life-changing.

AN INFANT'S CHOICE
In November 1985 in a greatly altered state of awareness, I re-experienced an event from my infancy. As mentioned elsewhere in this book, whether or not this event actually occurred in my infancy during this present incarnation is immaterial. The important aspect of it is that my soul utilized this particular way to bring about important growth and healing at a deep, cellular level.

I am 3 days old and well aware that the people around me in my new earth family do not remember who they are -- they are unaware of their limitless spiritual, divine nature. Like most of humanity, these well-meaning people have adopted family and cultural beliefs that human beings are finite, weak, helpless victims of circumstances. Life to them is primarily a physical experience, with little emphasis on the mental or emotional nature and very little awareness of the spiritual nature. As an unlimited soul in a 3-day-old baby body, I feel imprisoned and very constricted in this psychic space.

Feeling much anguish, I am weeping and pouring out my heart to the God Presence, "They don't remember who they are and, therefore, they cannot possibly see who I am, so I don't want to stay here. I won't be able to retain all of my consciousness if I stay here. I will have to begin shutting down some of my awareness and adopt some of these limited beliefs in order to survive here."

At this time, God and I are still one energy field. I am still greatly identified with the soul, but I have also become individuated and am now primarily located in a separate container. I am still fully aware of the God Presence that is right here with me and know that I am part of that energy field. The contact and communication with it still flows easily back and forth but my containment now feels confining and I am afraid I will begin to feel more separate from God.

I feel enormous sadness and anguish for I sense that an even greater separation will occur if I stay in

this body. My family, unfortunately, is more or less
under the influence of both a religion and culture
which focus on the negative attributes of sin, con-
demnation and judgment rather than on the vast,
limitless nature of spirit, the joy of life and the
inestimable bliss of the soul. Fear, not love, domi-
nates the group consciousness. The focus on fear is
not even questioned in this cultural milieu. They all
have so fully accepted this way of life that they are
not even aware the fear is there. But in my newborn
state, a newly-washed soul fresh from the ethereal
realms of light which have been my abode before
this lifetime, I feel the negative energy of those
limiting beliefs encasing me like a straitjacket. (This
experience alone taught me that the ultimate agony
is to be separated in consciousness from the God
Presence of Love and Light.)*

*In our true identity as Souls we never can *really* be separated from God, but we can,
through loss of consciousness, close the door to the God Presence and forget our
true identity. This can be likened to a royal prince who falls into a deep sleep,
develops amnesia and wanders off into a foreign land. He wakes up alone, cold,
injured, hungry and quite unaware that he is suffering from amnesia. Because of the
unfortunate circumstances in which he finds himself, he concludes that he is a
pauper. Other amnesiacs around him concur with his erroneous beliefs. Although
he is still a royal prince who already has more riches than he will ever need, he may
wander in misery for long years.

If a traveller comes along who recognizes him and tries to tell him who he really
is, he may not believe that person and may even decide that the traveller is insane.
In reality, all the prince need do is begin to listen and accept the possibility that he
may be more than he thinks he is and that his mistaken notions and acceptance of
limitations have been made up entirely in his own mind as a result of basing his
identity on his circumstances. As soon as he begins to believe even the *possibility*
that his identity may be different than he thinks, he has begun returning to his home
of abundance and grandeur.

Continuing the dialogue with the energy Presence - with God - I cry and plead, "I don't want to stay here. I can't hang on to all my consciousness if I stay here. I'm not going to stay here."

God's response is calm and certain, without coercion or bias of any kind: "You didn't come here for you."

Confused, I asked, "Then why am I here?"

While enveloping me in a feeling of indescribable safety and love, the God Presence answers, patient as eternity, "You came here to love."*

This statement made me realize that, regardless of the oppressively strong personal fears which were stimulating my desire to return home to the world of spirit, my true soul purpose for being in this body was "to love." While this was my "assignment," it was taken on voluntarily. It is really more accurate to say that this was a self-assignment, for even as the God Presence and the soul are one, any directive from God is also from the Self. I knew at the time that I had freely chosen to take on this embodiment. The energy field of the God Presence remained with me, as me, but the dialogue regarding my "leaving" had been settled.

---

*Later I noticed that, only three days after birth, I had already begun to forget the purpose about which I was clear when I undertook this semester in another human body. Is it any wonder, then, that usually an adult human being not only has no conscious recall of his real purpose for this lifetime, but he may have no awareness whatsoever that the soul ever had a purpose at all. When a person does begin to attune to the soul, a great elation occurs which warms his whole life.

Later as I thought about the assignment, "You came here to love," I realized that choosing to love in all circumstances would certainly provide a powerfully effective environment for my own learning. I, therefore, had no thought that the words, "You didn't come here for you" meant that I, personally, had nothing to learn. Rather, an attitude was conveyed that to focus on self and personal desires *alone* would be the slowest way to learn. Indeed an intention to love under all circumstances would provide the most fertile matrix for individual growth.

If I had chosen to leave my body at three days old, no physical cause would have been responsible and my family could not have known by ordinary means why I "died." I feel that it may have been a case of Sudden Infant Death Syndrome (SIDS), which is a phenomenon that takes the lives of many healthy children from birth to one year of age.

Whether a vision or other numinous event seems to be from the present lifetime, as above, or a kind of composite experience drawn from beyond time, as in the one immediately below, the soul always utilizes the exact method which will bring about maximum healing in its own perfect time and way. The following vision occurred on March 22, 1985, and continues to be one of the most liberating of my entire life. I am very glad that I was keeping a journal for I wrote this account soon afterward.

ALL MY PARENTS

Paramahansa Yogananda is standing here before me singing an ancient Sanskrit chant which is familiar to me. In a powerful yet very sweet voice, he sings,

> "No birth, no death, no caste have I
> Father, mother, have I none
> I am He, I am He
> Blessed Spirit, I am He"

Suddenly in front of me I see hundreds of men and women, paired as couples and standing in a long, undulating line in a sloping, green meadow. These people are of every race, color and nationality I can imagine, dressed in a great variety of costumes from places all over the world. The stunning realization comes to me that all of these people are my parents. They are couples who have been my physical parents from the beginning of my experiences in embodiments until now. At the very beginning of the line, three couples stand in the shadows. They are Stone Age people and are not very conscious or 'awake.'

My attention is most powerfully drawn to the next couple. They are Egyptian and are the focal point of this entire long line of people. They are standing in full, bright sunlight, dressed in flowing, white clothing, tall and dignified, regal in bearing. I realize they have been very important to me for my soul learned a lot in the incarnation as the child of this couple, making a giant leap in consciousness during that embodiment. I feel reverence, humility, awe, love and great appreciation for the part they played in moving me along so rapidly in that lifetime.

Moving forward from the Egyptians, there are many people dressed in a wide array of costumes. Here are couples who lived in ancient times, during the time of Jesus and afterward down through the centuries, into the Middle Ages and the Victorian era. Here are Greeks, Jews, Polynesians, Blacks, Orientals, Anglo-Saxons, rich people, poor people, people dressed in the most elaborate tapestries and velvets, people wearing hats and headdresses wonderful and peculiar almost beyond imagination, people dressed in the simplest homespun cloth and people who wear nothing at all. The last two people in the line are my present parents. I am astonished to realize that they are not more significant to me in this frame of reference than any other couple in the long line of people.

I move along the line, making strong connections with certain ones. I stop and gaze into the eyes of a large, heavy-browed and bearded, beautiful man who is dressed in an indigo velveteen jacket, trimmed with gold threads. He is English and wears a luxurious four-sided cap which matches his jacket and is pinched at the crown, flaring out to form a kind of square. He wears it nonchalantly. It strikes me that this cap seems very foreign and ethnic to me, and at the same time it seems as familiar as everyday. This man, my father in some lifetime, communicates through his eyes that he loved me and expressed his love for me, his dark-haired daughter, as best he knew how. This was a revelation to me for I had thought he was hardly aware of my existence and had suffered that whole lifetime with the struggle for assurance of his paternal affection. Not a word is spoken between us, but healing energy moves back and forth in our gaze as we experience that each is sure of the other's love. At this moment it seems needless to think of forgiveness for there is no longer anything to forgive.

I continue the movement along the line, connecting with other 'parents' and realize that all of them have done their very best. I know, finally, that although some of them made mistakes which had been painful to me as their child, those mistakes were all in ignorance; none was a malicious, knowing act. These people love me and I love them so much! There is nothing left to forgive between any of us. All perceived debts are now erased, all inequities now balanced. It feels complete. I see that all events in all these lives have taught me in one way or another, helping me to evolve to my present stage of consciousness. The process of connecting with them now seems finished and I back up, moving away from the line, but keeping my gaze fixed on them.

Yogananda has been standing nearby throughout this whole experience and, though I do not take my eyes off all my parents, I am aware that Jesus Christ is now standing beside him and says, "I am from everlasting to everlasting, from beginning to end." I stand gazing at this long line of couples as a lightning-fast streak of radiant white light, like a meteorite with a little tail, enters the first couple in the line and moves through every one of them at the level of the heart. It is the Light of Superconsciousness and I remember the words of Christ, referring to the Spirit which filled him, "I am the Light of the world."(St. John 9:5)

I realize that this Light is my true parent and that each of these couples, beloved as they are, only gave me a body as I moved through these families. These are my *physical* parents only, not my *spiritual* parents. My true, spiritual parent is that Light. This energy is the soul, and this vision is showing me that my essence is divine, just as the essence of each human being is divine. I realize that I have never been alone, that the Divine energy has been with me in unbroken continuity throughout all these embodiments, watching over me through these earth parents all along the way.*

---

*Any thought or feeling that I was alone or unloved stemmed solely from the separation of my conscious awareness from the spirit part of me. Like a toddler who cries as though his heart is breaking because mother leaves for a few minutes and will ultimately be consoled only by the presence of mother herself, so it is with us. We feel alone, abandoned and unloved until the reunion with our own divine essence, whereupon we blissfully realize that we have never been alone.

The group in the line now communicates with me telepathically: "We have been channels for the Divine in your life, quickening your evolution through the love in our families. You now can be a channel of love for us, for many of us are presently in physical form again. Realize that whenever you look into any pair of eyes, you may be gazing at one of us."

What a transformation came over me with that realization! I felt a burning desire to be an instrument for their liberation. Since that time I have gazed into so many different pairs of eyes with the awareness that at some time or another the soul into whose eyes I gaze may have loved me unconditionally. In some lifetime I could even have been their precious newborn infant — or they mine.

One could easily ask, "Were all these people actually your parents in various incarnations or is this just your imagination?" My response to this is that to the extent that a person thinks or believes it is true, to that extent it *is* true. If you *think* something happened or if it *actually* happened, the result is the same anyway in that the same neurological changes are effected in the brain in both instances. In this case, I received enormous benefit and tremendous healing and have little curiosity about such details. If a practical purpose such as this is served, then much good is achieved. In my experience, it makes no difference whether my teacher stands in front of me in a physical form and gives me vital information or appears inwardly, giving that same information.

This visionary experience left me with the knowingness that anytime we truly love, our spiritual evolution is speeded up. It also brought deep healing at a core energy level and completed much of my attachment to my present parents. I still love them as much as ever, but instead of viewing them solely as my mom and dad, I am much more able to see their transcendent identities as two precious souls who lovingly volunteered to be my parents in this incarnation and who, like me, are on earth to evolve according to their own free-will choices. Most of my needs are satisfied by the spiritual joy and peace I feel within, so I am free of any obsessive need to make my present human family fit into any preconceived mold I might otherwise have wanted to insist upon and am more peaceful finding enjoyment in the perfection of their unique expressions.

Realization of and surrender to the role my soul wants to play in this incarnation enables me to be a more supportive member of my human family. People sometimes fear that mystical or spiritual experiences can lead to impractical or undesirable results. In my experience, however, quite the opposite is true. My effectiveness in family, business and personal relationships has been decidedly enhanced.

This liberating perspective enables me to be more available to spirit for its creative expression and more available to my family, too. Of course, I now realize that what I was seeking all along is the relationship with God. I was reflecting on this recently during a walk in the park and the following poem wrote itself in my mind:

I HAVE BEEN SEARCHING FOR THEE

It is You, Beloved, who has loved me through each nurturing
Earth mother and, when one of my mothers failed,
It was You who collapsed the illusion,
So I would seek through the pain to find Thee.

It was Your strength guiding me through each wise
Earth father and, through the hurt of each weak father,
It was You who whispered,
"Don't stop here! Look for Me. Look for Me."

Then I felt Your love in the embrace of my lover
And I thought I was home at last
Oh! My heart broke when that illusion ended
And slipped into the past.

I felt You move in my forming baby,
Then You smiled through her newborn gaze
But You go on playing hide and seek
And I search for You in this maze.

Oh! My Beloved, hiding from me
You fly the birds in the air, swim the fish in the sea,
You blow in the wind and sway in this tree,
...pound the heart in my chest, yet You still hide from me.

Now I see You, now I don't
How long must this go on?
I'm exhausted with hunger and searching and cold
And impatient to get back home.

Please open this door and receive me
Oh! I dream of nothing else.
And until you hold me in your arms
I'll just wait right here on these steps.

Spiritual aspirants from many different cultures and times reach this same place of loving their family devotedly, but become ready to move beyond the exclusive attachment to one human family in order to embrace the greater family. With this shift in awareness, one comes to realizations such as those expressed in this quatrain from the Mahabharata, India's ancient classic story:

Tvameva mata cha pita tvameva	Thou alone are mother and father to me
Tvameva bandhu cha sakha tvameva	Thou alone are kin and friend to me
Tvameva vidya dravinam tvameva	Thou alone are knowledge and wealth to me
Tvameva sarvam mama deva deva.	Thou art my all, My God of Gods.

DIVINE VISITATIONS

Some visions would more rightly be called *visitations*. From time to time, I have been aware of the vibrant presences of Babaji, Yogananda and Jesus Christ. On other occasions, I have heard only an inner voice or sensed a divine presence without the aspect of a specific personality. Some of Walt Whitman's writings seem to indicate similar experiences, for he referred to the expanded state as "My Soul," but also spoke of it as though it were another person. In addition, Francis Bacon consistently referred to the expansion in his own consciousness as another person. (See Cosmic Consciousness by Richard Maurice Bucke.) It is my understanding that when such a remarkable event occurs, the conscious mind is sufficiently quiet to allow the vivid experience. This can happen during meditation, rebirthing, or at other times when the door from the unconscious is open as a result of other stimuli, such as that experienced during times of overwhelming grief.

I also feel that spiritual attunement and devotion are key ingredients. These traits soften the heart and help an individual become more willing and able to be still and listen. In the same way that sunlight can shine into a room only if windows or doors are open, visions and visitations ordinarily occur only in people who are open and receptive. Just as in conventional human relationships, these wonderful, loving, powerful personages will usually visit only those who have invited them.

Such divine beings are not confined to solitary, physical bodies as ordinary humans are. Instead, they participate in a much higher and more expanded order of reality where they are not necessarily separate one from the other. Manifesting in the third dimension, they are more accurately described as "light beings," since this pure state of electrical essence is most often the way they appear. Attempts to fit such mystical experiences into the lower order usually only result in confusion. Perhaps we can learn to be more accepting of them and, if we need to evaluate them, do so by observing the results they achieve in the third-dimensional world.

A VISION IN THE DESERT

The following vision occurred in 1985 during a deep meditation at my home in Encinitas, California.

In a flash I no longer feel located in my carpeted meditation room but instead am standing in a huge, expanse of desert in Central Mexico. (I have no idea why or how I know this but am certain of this location.) Jagged purple-blue mountains loom in the far distance all around this parched, flat place. I am standing in the very center of the hub of a wheel whose spokes radiate out in all directions. Thousands of people are approaching the hub where I am standing, as though they are converging along those spokes. I look at the ground, which is sand-colored and nearly free of vegetation, and notice that I cannot see a wheel or spokes. Then I realize that this wheel is an "energy structure" — this experience is occurring in *energy!*

I stand watching these people walk toward me. Some are now very near and thousands of others are still some distance away. As the first ones come close enough for me to see their facial features, I recognize that they look like the Indians who live in Mexico around the vicinity of San Miguel de Allende. My attention is sharply drawn to one little woman. Her face looks like a deeply-lined copper mask. She appears to be about middle-age with coal-black hair parted in the middle and braided down the back. She stoops slightly, looking mostly at the ground and carries a cloth-bound pack on her back. It seems to me that her stooping is more of an attitude than a response to the physical weight of her relatively small burden. Compared to most Caucasians, she is very tiny, as are the others.

For the first time, my inner voice speaks, "See how small they are; they are the size of children. Spiritually they are like children also, but when they receive the unconditional love of mother, it will stimulate their spiritual growth."

My heart swells with tremendous love. I feel the misery of their hopelessness and the pain of their poverty. I am nearly overwhelmed with this burden of suffering. I am then drawn straight upward in a shaft of golden white light to a higher wheel, which appears to be the same shape as the wheel below, except this higher wheel is so full of radiant light, it is almost blinding. In the upper wheel there is a multitude of angelic light beings, who are playing and buoyantly moving about as though weightless and completely carefree. My own body is like that of an infant, except it is made of light.

Standing in the light-filled center of the upper hub are Jesus and Yogananda. They hold me as one holds a small infant. I feel puzzled and astonished but also entirely safe and joyful. I begin to feel that it is okay to take everything very lightly, that regardless of how painful and grievous events and circumstances below may appear, nothing is so serious after all. These light-filled throngs of beings are singing a song that utterly fills the whole infinite space. Its tones are incredibly beautiful, as though the music is alive and generative. I feel it as much as I hear it. I would describe it as highly oxygenated, although I do not know what oxygen has to do with sound.

From this fourth-dimensional place of light, we all can see the entire scene below: the energy wheel and its spokes, the hub where my physical body still stands and the thousands of people walking across the sandy, flat plain of the desert to converge on the hub — *but none of those below can see us or the light-filled scene above.*

I am clearly aware that the energy which enlivens the people and activities in the scene below emanates directly from the intense light and the luminous presences in the scene above. This higher level is focusing energy to the humans on the earth below, although they are unaware of it.

These scenes then disappeared from my inner view as instantly as they had appeared. However, the aspect of my consciousness that was lifted up the shaft to the upper wheel was somehow left there. Although my awareness came fully back into my body in the carpeted room in my home, I did not feel at all the same as before. The experience had created an expanded state within that allowed me to retain the energy memory of the lightness and perfection that is occurring on the higher level. This perfection can flow to the lower level - into an individual life - to the extent that one is able to lift his consciousness by developing a receptive attitude, taking his eyes off the ground and looking upward symbolically.

Apparently this vision was very important for it recurred several times over a month-long period in 1985. I felt intuitively that my energy field was being cleansed and expanded to enable me to see a higher purpose and greater potential than I could have seen before. and in the years since this experience, I have found that I frequently am able to see and feel the higher, light-filled, dimension of a situation, even when others around me may be completely caught up in the drama of earth events.

I became acutely aware of this phenomenon when I first began conducting workshops. A person displaying a particularly petty, self-centered personality trait was among the participants, and others in the group were visibly annoyed. *Normally*, I would have been annoyed, too, however, I realized with astonishment and delight that all I felt for the person was compassion and love. Remarkably, my only response was that which a loving mother might feel towards her toddler. Such a parent would realize that her little one would outgrow his childish traits and she could, therefore, lovingly and patiently provide the psychic and emotional latitude for him to mature beyond his egocentricity. It was as if I was no longer limited by the small personality self and that some expanded, superintelligent, superloving presence was expressing through me. I did not have to "try" to respond patiently to the person in my class; I did not have to remind myself to be compassionate. As new as the experience was for me, I did not have to rationalize it at all. I just noticed that my automatic response was supportive, patient and loving. Such enhanced interpersonal ability is not an unusual result when transpersonal consciousness becomes the norm in a person's life through spiritual evolution.

A RE-BONDING WITH JESUS

According to my journal, the following ecstatic vision occurred on a Sunday afternoon in February 1985:

> I am on a high jungle plateau, somewhere in Mexico or South America. The vegetation is tropical - abundant, lush and green - and towering trees form an umbrella above. The dense foliage creates a semi-darkness and it feels humid but very pleasant. There is a small natural pool like a tiny lagoon; it seems appealing and I am going to get into it. This place looks like it would be a natural habitat for snakes and, because of this, I am surprised that I feel no fear. Nude now, I slip down into the dark water, which feels soft and soothing to my skin. It seems important to completely submerge and I move down until the water covers my head.
>
> Now I feel strong hands, one under each of my arms, lifting me straight up and out of the water. Though no one else was present with me before I entered the pool, I feel safe and unstartled. As I quickly open my eyes to see who is lifting me, I am gazing into the softest eyes I have ever seen and a face which is so indescribably gentle and full of compassion that it takes my breath away. This is *Jesus!* He is about six feet tall and wears a long white robe. I feel so merged with His energy that I am almost unaware of my separateness. Remarkably, this experience does not seem overwhelming or awesome to me while it is occurring.

Jesus has not spoken audibly but we are in perfect telepathic rapport. Moving quietly, He places a white robe over my head and I insert my hands and arms into its sleeves.

It is rather loose and the hem falls easily to my feet. He kisses me seven times, symbolically opening the seven cerebro-spinal energy centers. I feel such sweetness that it is like melting. Jesus! *My Jesus!* He has re-bonded with me.

Only now do I realize that there has been distance between us for a period of some years. Throughout my childhood and teen years, I was utterly in love with Jesus. Every day after my inner experience with Him at age 14 in high school, I had a constant inner dialogue with Him. He was my teacher, my closest companion, my master, my God. I felt so close to Him. I used to pray one prayer over and over again: "Oh, Master, please keep me with you. Please let me die rather than take even one step away from you." This inner communion sustained me. I never got into adolescent or teen trouble of any kind because I had this utter in-love-ness going on inside.

At the end of my teen years, I broke away from the fundamentalist church I had attended with my family for I had become uncomfortable with a theology that focused on sin and judgment instead of loving acceptance. Without realizing it, however, I had left some of my connection with Jesus, too. Like having arsenic laced in with mother's milk, it was difficult to separate the toxic dogma from the divine love. And now, today, Jesus has re-bonded with me. I have come full circle.

Jesus and I walk together out of this area and quickly down the mountain to a grassy meadow below. Night has fallen and ahead of us there are four or five young men around a campfire. Nearby are the animals they are tending. (I am not sure if they are cattle or sheep or maybe they are llamas.) As we approach the group of youths, I realize that, although Jesus and I can see them, they cannot see us. One dark-skinned youth of about 17 years old with coal-black hair is standing at the head of the fire. He appears to be talking to the others, who are seated around the fire, but I cannot hear what he is saying. Jesus moves around behind him and places His left arm around this young man, who is now standing between us, yet unaware that we are there. Jesus taps with His right index finger on the young man's chest over the heart and, looking directly into my eyes, speaks to me audibly for the first time, "This is how I work — one heart at a time."

With that, the vision ended. I have no idea how long it lasted; it could have been two minutes or twenty minutes or forty minutes. All I know is that a flood of realization had entered my being and I was transformed once again. Practical and healing, this miraculous, preternatural experience brought many positive benefits. I feel the vital energy of this vision frequently for its memory surfaces just at the moment when it is most relevant.

THE ONE DOOR OUT

About five o'clock one morning in June 1986, I was seated on a low, kneeling bench in my meditation room. I began to feel an unusually powerful energy which felt like Babaji's vibration. I am unable to adequately convey the thrill and peace of His presence. He stayed with me for what seemed like a long time that morning and directed a whole visionary experience in which it felt like my brain was "re-wired."

In this vision, Babaji took me on a journey, showing me a broad avenue lined with palatial estates. The residents were expending all of their time and energy on the pursuit and enjoyment of wealth. I could see that the end of this long, beautiful street was a dead end, for there was "no door out," as I was told telepathically. We then went down a different street, where all the people were pursuing fame, but this street also led to a dead end. Then He took me down a dirt road where pitifully poor shanties and lean-to buildings cluttered the sides of the road. Babaji told me (telepathically) that the people on this road were "pretending to be poor just as the people on the first avenue were pretending to be rich." I felt a deep, inner realization that, as divine souls, we *always* choose what we want or need somehow, even though we may consciously forget *why* we made a certain choice and it may *appear* that we have no choice in some life situations. Once an individual awakens from the stupor of self-conscious life, he realizes that he has been playing a role.

Finally, we reached the end of the dirt road and it, too, was a dead end. This was not the way out either. Then I looked up and saw a door — the one door out. I exited through that door and God was there waiting for me with my seat saved, and I knew that it had been there for me since the first time I left "home," when I began all these rounds of incarnations. I had been safe all this time, through all the wonderfully happy and dreadfully painful circumstances, no matter how alone I had felt or how frightened I had been at times. I also clearly saw that there is *no other door.*

After this experience, I felt a calm realization that the only way to graduate from earth life is through spiritual evolution. There is no trap door. There is no lake of fire into which a loving God, turned brutal, throws his erring offspring. Ultimately, there is no other place that one can go other than home to God. A human being keeps repeating lifetime after lifetime, learning more each round until he evolves sufficiently to find the one door that leads out. It is all like a big movie.

After that morning, many personal attachments fell away and I gained deep understandings about how divine souls in human bodies learn needed lessons in the schoolhouse we call earth. I felt more detachment regarding a number of human situations which had been painful before. I feel a deep compassion for humans experiencing tragedy, but, since this experience, have less of a tendency to feel engulfed in others' pain. This allows me to be supportive without feeling that I am drowning in others' emotional material.

BAPTISM OF FIRE

Later in 1986, I was home alone one night, spending time silently and unaware that one of the most extraordinary events of my life was about to occur. The end of a close personal relationship seemed imminent and, although I felt this was for the best, I also felt extremely sad about its demise. Sinking into a state of deep reflection, I began thinking about Babaji, longing to go to the Himalayas to be with Him, where I thought I might be safe from heartache. I then felt the expansion of my heart center, a familiar experience, accompanied by a terrific amount of energy both in my body and seemingly in the entire room. I realized, suddenly, that Babaji was present. Sad no longer, my whole awareness quickly became absorbed in the vibrant ecstasy of His vibration. On this occasion, Babaji was not visible to me, but His presence was as unmistakable as a sudden, cool breeze on a scorching summer day, no less a blessing because invisible. Unable to sit still due to the inordinate amount of energy coursing through me, I paced the floor and poured out my heart to Him, laughing and crying in a rapture so intense that I could only think of it later as "excruciating joy!"

Because of the tremendous electrical vibration present during this visitation, I felt closer to being overwhelmed than at any other time in my life. My body "burned" from head to toe, as though every cell was on fire and I realized that I was being purified. I felt like I was dying but in the presence of such indescribable love, I was not afraid.

After this experience, I kept hearing the words, "excruciating joy," realizing that they do not make sense in combination with each other. I looked up "excruciating" in the dictionary and found that "ex" is a prefix representing the outside, the exterior of a thing, and "cruc" means "to crucify." An immediate intuitive understanding came into my mind: the joyous energy which I felt so profoundly when Babaji was present that night had been crucifying the outer shell of ego. Like a rock-hard mud wall begins dissolving in a torrential downpour, some of my ego, most assuredly, was dissolving in the intense vibration of Babaji's presence.

SNOW MOUNTAIN

In August 1989, during an hour of intense breathwork with four other people, I experienced an unforgettable vision which gave me specific direction regarding work I was to do.

I am taken to a place high above the mountains of Colorado; a multitude of magnificent higher presences fills the whole space. The feeling in this place is nothing less than ethereal joy. Everything in the whole vicinity — below me on the mountains and above — is snow white.

A cloak and headdress of snow white feathers is then placed around a woman who is representative of Divine Mother. Luminous presences fill the whole area and at the end of this visionary experience, hundreds of baby white birds are being born. As I see

and feel the easy birthing of these precious little ones
out of this matrix of unconditional love, I am told,
telepathically, that they are snow white baby eagles
who "know they can fly."

The symbology is clear to me: the people who will
come to the snowy, mountainous place will awaken
to a full experience of their true identity as pure,
unlimited children of God. They will begin to remember who they are and find attunement with the
soul.

When my awareness returned to a more ordinary state of
consciousness, I knew that I must schedule a training somewhere in the Colorado mountains to serve the awakening of
many people, as I was shown. The others who had been in the
room with me said that they had seen white light all around
and flowing through me during this vision. Even though I
had not spoken yet and they did not know, therefore, the
specific details of my inner experience, all four of them
reported that they had seen this "whiteness" and felt the
presence of the higher energies.

Two days later in a very synchronistic way, I became aware
of a resort called Snow Mountain, Colorado (which I had
never even heard of until after this vision) and I made
reservations for a week-long training to be held a few months
later in January of 1990.

Forty-seven people from around the United States came to
this workshop, most of whom I had not met before. Although
introductions were scheduled for the first session, even

before they began, one individual experienced a spontaneous rebirth. Other people began making similar break-
throughs that same evening, and the entire week became a
time of glorious awakening. To say that it was life-changing
seems an understatement for all of us. It was a playful, joyful
homecoming to the rapturous, childlike love of the heart.

During those days, we all began to feel like a family, and
that bond continues to be strong. As this familial love expanded, some of us spontaneously imagined our circle becoming vastly larger, to encompass everyone on our beloved
Mother Earth.

With the entire mountain blanketed by a swirling, protective blizzard, we gathered in the huge octagonal chapel at
Snow Mountain. Holding hands in graceful concentric circles,
we danced the Dance of Remembrance to the time-worn
tones of a Peruvian flute, moving in quiet tempo and silently
looking into each other's eyes. As we continued our rhyth-
mic steps to the musical cadence, spontaneous memories of
timeless relationships - of ancient sacred bondedness one to
another - arose from deep within. Afterwards, a sweet awareness remained that each pair of eyes into which we might
ever gaze could evoke another precious memory of loving
connectedness.

About mid-week, a brilliant artist, who was our youngest
participant, painted a rainbow-colored poster and placed it
on the wall. A heartfelt expression for many beautiful newborn snow white eagles, it stated simply, "I was born at Snow
Mountain!"

The Inner Light

In the center of my being, an inner light resides. This light was my abode before I entered the fertilized cell in the womb of my mother and began directing the formation of a little baby body. As I floated in amniotic fluid, this light continuously bathed my whole being in love and perfect joy. I was one with my mother and all of life.

Breath became my lifeline after birth and I gradually attuned my awareness to the people of my family and this world. They were asleep, dreaming dreams of limitation and darkness. I fell asleep, too, until the pain of imagined separation from my home of love and light became intense enough to wake me up.

Awakening, now, all fear and thought of pain are leaving. This perfect love has been here all along, waiting for me to open the door again to feel its radiant, healing warmth. I bathe in pools of golden, liquid light. I am home again.

Playing my part in this dream drama becomes easier for now I remember that I am in school and this is a stage. I can see beyond the dreams and realize that costumes worn and identities pretended could never change who we really are. They are only for learning.

I keep open the door of the inner light. Love saturates my being and pours through to other students on this stage. Sleeping members of this beloved earth family, long tormented by the nightmares they dream so real, are awakening one by one, elated to realize that this joy and love, this inner light, has been ever here awaiting our homecoming.

6

Listening to the Soul

"And thine ears shall hear a word behind thee, saying, 'This is the way, walk ye in it.'"   **Isaiah 30:21**

There is a voice deep within each human being which emanates directly from the soul. It can be heard as clearly as outer sounds can be heard. The existence of this phenomenal voice is as ancient as the human race, but for many centuries the awareness and experience of it has greatly declined. In today's society, if you talk to God, it is called prayer, but if God talks to you, it is called psychosis! Regardless of society's ignorance of divine response, however, anyone who has had this experience knows that Isaiah's message is as current and applicable for an awakened person today as it was when it was written. This inner voice is the soul attempting to communicate with the conscious mind, striving to awaken the individual to realize his true identity as a divine being and recall his own unique purpose for this incarnation.

You can learn to tune in to the intuitive awareness of the soul for guidance, healing, creative ideas, harmonious solutions to problems and for many other purposes. This ability is inherent in you as part of your birthright. It is programmed into your circuitry. Its development will tremendously improve the quality of your life for it is like having a brilliant, loving genius always available to help and advise you. This may seem like an overstatement to you but it is actually a gross understatement of reality. Contact and harmony with your soul will provide everything you are seeking and more.

Initial attempts to attune to the soul's messages could be compared to scanning across a radio dial to pick up a station. When the antenna is clearly aligned to the transmitter, the signal will come in free of static. The life force energy of the soul within you contains living information and when you learn to attune to it, you will have discovered the ultimate guidance mechanism built into your circuitry by life itself.

A human being is unique among all the creatures of the earth because he is the only one capable of expressing full divinity. Located in the human brain and along the spinal column are the seven very sensitive chakras which are present in no other creature. These centers function somewhat like electrical transformers, receiving power from the Universal Energy Field, that vast vibrational ocean around you, and converting it for your use.

The amount of energy which you can receive and the way it is expressed depends to a great extent on the evolutionary development of these cerebrospinal centers. Just as a fifth grader can consciously absorb more mental information than he could as a kindergartener, a person who grows and evolves in consciousness is capable of receiving a higher vibration of spiritual power than he could at an earlier stage.

Most often, the voice of the Soul is the voice of conscience. In many people, however, it is silent because over a period of a lifetime or perhaps many lifetimes it has been ignored.

Without the direct link to the soul, a person becomes increasingly unfeeling.

Many people today are very disconnected from the feelings of their own conscience. Observe the emotional and physical violence which are marketed so successfully as "entertainment" in today's society. A person of natural sensitivity feels sickened by even a glimpse of such offensive material, while one who is disconnected from the soul can sit in a theatre munching popcorn while the gore on the screen becomes bloodier and bloodier. Such a person is defended not only against any compassionate feeling for another person, but literally cannot even feel his own feelings. He tells himself that he is not bothered by such subject matter when in truth he may unconsciously be seeking something shocking enough to pierce through many layers of defense to his own inner feelings.

As an individual begins to respond to the soul, he becomes increasingly uncomfortable with untruths or other deceptive behavior. Living without integrity finally becomes downright painful. More frequently, now, he chooses right behavior and right attitude in his life and that inner voice of conscience grows stronger and louder. Instead of relying solely on external values, he trusts this inner presence more and begins to listen to its messages.

He now can claim more of his own inner power, not as a force to be used over other people, but as the ability to know his own truth and face any consequence of his honest, autonomous choices. Whereas in the past, he may have looked solely to others for advice, seeking safety in logic alone, he now begins to hear the superior wisdom of the soul also.

The rational mind plots its actions like moves in a chess game, but the soul sees multi-dimensionally. Not only is this form of intelligence superior to the logical mind, it is also much more efficient. To analyze a situation and make a decision from a rational point of view (often in denial or ignorance of the powerful emotional content beneath) is time consuming and exhausting. Afterwards, you may still feel uncertain and anxious, for the conscious mind is dominated by the little ego which is separate, afraid and utterly defensive.

The ego tries to outsmart others and manipulate the odds. It knows its limitations but boasts loud and long, intending to convince any listener of its superiority. The person caught in the ego's fear will feel afraid and depressed (if he allows himself to feel anything at all) and others around him will feel uncomfortable also.

The process of attuning to the soul's direction is usually lightning fast and leaves one with a sense of serenity and renewed trust in life itself. The rational mind will argue that it is too time consuming to pay attention to inner feelings; it will insist on weighing evidence and basing a decision on past occurrences. While it is okay to evaluate such information, relying solely on rational evaluation is a slower and less certain road to travel than following intuition.

YOUR SOUL WILL GUIDE YOU

When you can tune in to the wisdom of the soul, you will know exactly what to do, without analysis and without benefit of substantiating statistics from past events and anticipated future trends. If you realize that you are wearing yourself out agonizing over some decision, it may help to stop and remember this:

Your mission,
should you decide to accept it,
is to find out what your Soul
wants you to do
and *do it!*

Oftentimes the inner presence will speak, using certain specific terms, but intending so much more than those mere words convey. It is as though Spirit utilizes certain language to provide some stimulation within the brain and much additional information is then transmitted telepathically in the form of knowingness. At such times, there is no doubt regarding true meaning. This form of information always resonates congruently at every level. Sometimes the expanded meaning or message of such an inner communication will unfold over days, weeks or even months.

The soul is ever perfect and needs no improvement. It could be compared to a pure gold statue, perfect in every way, which has been covered over by layer upon layer of mud. The task in such a case would be to wash away those layers to reveal the perfection always there. Whether you are feeling powerless and victimized or shining in the radiance of soul realization, your essential identity remains the same. The ultimate plan for spiritual evolution is through free choice. God never takes away free will and as much as the Divine hungers for your reunion with the soul, it is you who will choose when it will occur.

Throughout many incarnations, it could be said that the soul takes only an impersonal interest in the mundane activities of an individual life. When an individual has chosen a path of discipline and growth, willing through continual self-observation to work on mining the gold of his own potential, there comes a point when the soul takes a very direct interest in that person's life.

When you listen to the voice within, it will become clearer and stronger. As you proceed slowly, individuating your own authentic feelings with great self-honesty, you build an inner strength. The power of self-knowledge is recognized in the word "Swami," a Sanskrit word which means "he who is one with himself." Just as "a house divided against itself...cannot stand," (Mark 3:25) so a person who is not aligned with himself, through awareness of his feelings and attunement with the soul, cannot be peaceful and powerful.

The soul will usually communicate guidance *to* you *for* you. It is wise to be cautious about receiving messages either for or from other people. The ego mind is fraught with many tricks and delusions and can get very inflated with power and control over others. It loves to think that it knows more than others, but each human being is here to learn to tune in to his own soul for himself, without depending on another individual.

LEARNING TO TRUST YOUR INNER SELF

Never forego your own discrimination and your own common sense. If you have a gut-level feeling about something, it probably would be wise to heed it or at least proceed cautiously and observe from a place of neutrality a little longer before taking action. When the soul is truly communicating with you, the information will make perfect sense and will leave you feeling alive and peaceful, loving and enthusiastic. The soul will never direct you to do something that will bring disgrace or shame to yourself or another. Do your best to be completely honest with yourself, without ulterior motive, as you seek attunement with and guidance from your soul.

Children play a game where the one who is "it" searches for a hidden object. If he heads toward the hidden object, the others tell him that he is "getting hotter." When he moves in the wrong direction, the children shout, "You're getting colder!" In like fashion, as you take a first step, you may receive confirmation that you are headed in the right direction in the form of a surge of joy. That good feeling is the soul telling you that you are on track. Joseph Campbell called it "following your bliss." If, after you take a step, you feel depressed and anxious, that feeling may be the soul's way of saying, "Wrong way! Not this way!"

The soul uses these ways of communicating and it is up to you to learn to understand its signals. In the beginning stages, however, it is easy to confuse the voice of intuition with imagination. The only truth that can have meaning for you is that which resonates within your own being. The injunction to "know thyself" always applies, for when you continually check inside to find balance, you gradually become acquainted with yourself.*

USING DISCRIMINATION

Beginners sometimes confuse discernment with judgment but please be assured that discernment is an essential quality. Judgment occurs when you use a negative quality to label a person, as though this defines who that person is. Using discernment means that your conscious mind can tell good qualities from bad ones. It is easy to identify someone's bad behavior, for instance, but if you remember that a person can use his free will to choose differently at any moment and thus become a better person, it will allow him more latitude to make changes and you will feel better in the process, too.

Take full responsibility for any guidance you receive. It is never appropriate to repeat some message you may have heard and use a disclaimer such as, "Don't blame me! This is just what my guidance is telling me." If you ever feel like you are being urged to take an action which does not serve the highest good, it is wise to question it. It is your job to become

---

*The chart entitled "How to Evaluate Spiritual Communication," at the end of this chapter, can assist in this regard.

psychologically and emotionally healthy and integrated so you can be a capable instrument for the soul's expression. Being integrated means that you are fully responsible for everything you do and say, willing to face all consequences. When you achieve this, you are living your life in the light of your own soul. The most conscious kind of instrument is one who lives a life of spiritual integrity and has done the work necessary to receive communications from the soul in a conscious state.

BEING SURE COMMUNICATION IS FROM THE LIGHT

Just because a message comes from a non-physical source does not mean that it comes from the Light. The soul leaves the physical body at death and becomes a non-physical being, but the state of consciousness of that being is no greater after death than before, for death does not make a person suddenly better. Human beings make spiritual progress only while in physical form. The astral zone is the dwelling place of many souls (between embodiments), some of which are up to no good, just as they were up to no good *before* they left their last physical body. One person stated that her "guide" was an entity which was a pickpocket in its last incarnation. One might ask, "Are you interested in receiving 'wisdom' from a thief, whether in or out of a body?"

As in any learning process, it helps in the beginning to proceed slowly until you develop more skill and confidence. If you are uncertain about spiritual communications received through another person, you may gain more information by unemotionally observing the one who is speaking the communication and ask yourself: "Does this person live a pure life with high integrity, or is he selfishly motivated, interpersonally destructive, or willing to use force to manipulate others?" Remember that "...by their fruits ye shall know them." (Matt. 7:20) Do not become bedazzled by the financial success of such a person or by the great number of people who may congregate around him. Consensus is not the soul's way to evaluate. The Nazi movement in World War II Germany definitely had the majority of power, money and soldiers, but that did not make it right. Be clear that you are seeking only to know what the soul wants and you will then be closer to hearing its intuitive wisdom.

You are in a physical form to learn to become autonomous and directly in tune with your own soul, not to become dependent on another or surrender your free will. While you may receive assistance along the way, be aware that a true teacher always wants your own good and seeks ways to help you become empowered and autonomous.

In Zen Buddhism it is said that the role of a teacher is to preserve the student from the teacher's influence. One great teacher, who told his students not to believe anything he said, challenged them, instead, to put everything to the test in the laboratory of their own lives. That way, he said, each person would know whether or not a thing was true. When you have personal experience that has been tested in the crucible of your own life, you can truly use it, for then it is not mere belief but realization.

The purpose of spiritual communication is to help guide you along, like a healthy, intelligent, loving parent gently guides his child. Thus you gradually learn to think and function as the soul does. If you are meditating regularly and honestly doing your best, you will be guided to the right next step to take.

HOW TO EVALUATE SPIRITUAL COMMUNICATION

Communication from the Soul, the Higher Self and High Spiritual Levels

- For the highest good of all. Empowering to the receiver. The energy will feel positive, joyous, centered & happy.

- A focus on service to all. Emphasis on union and abundance. Inspires love, trust and peacefulness.

- Appeals to intelligence and aligns with common sense. Makes suggestions not demands. Never requires you to sacrifice your own free will. Never in conflict with high personal ethics.

- Specific direction. Guides you toward the next step *for you* - does not go too far ahead. Usually, you cannot utilize information which is beyond your next step.

- Clear, sometimes bold direction. Usually extremely brief; not wordy. Quite often you will hear or receive very few words along with a great knowingness that fills in the space between the lines. This is an unfolding of awareness from within and you will know *exactly* how to use it and where it fits in your life.

Communication from the Subconscious or Lower Astral Zones, Contaminated with Ego Desire and Illusion

- Slanted toward the good of the receiver and sometimes at others' expense. May create guilt, anxiety, urgency.

- May flatter ego. Creates specialness, exclusivity, glamour and separation.

- Unquestioning obedience and negation of one's free will may be demanded. May be in conflict with one's high personal standards, natural intelligence and common sense.

- Often is so general that it could apply to many situations or people (worded so that the 'psychic' will be 'right,' no matter what). Avoids specifics.

- May be lengthy and worded so cautiously that you find yourself confused about what is being communicated and the ego mind may hook you into self-scolding because you "should be able to understand it in the first place." If the little ego can distract you by bad feelings, you will be less likely to observe what is *really* going on.

7

The Way of Love

The path of love is the easiest —
it is the master key that unlocks all doors.
If you love enough, nothing will stand in your way.
                                    Christina Thomas

God is love and the plan for creation is rooted only in love. In order to feel any true happiness in life, we must have love. Love is the only healer ... the most important element in all of life ... the one indispensable. Whatever we love, love we must if we are to grow and evolve.

The object of love may not even matter so much, especially in the beginning, which helps us understand how many people go about selecting a marriage partner. A lady, for instance, may select a gentleman who clearly is not the kind of person she says she wants. She hides this clarity from herself until after the marriage, however, and soon begins complaining about his unacceptable traits.

If the lady had been willing and able to be really honest with herself, she would have been more aware of her own inner process. "I am aware that this man is not really the kind of partner I want," she might have said. "I am afraid, however, that I am not going to find one I *really* want who also wants me. If I am alone, I will not grow; in order to 'get into the game' of life, I must be married. I *must* get into this game, somehow, whether or not it is in an ideal way. Of course, I do not know how to verbalize all this, even to myself, so I will marry him and then pretend that I did not see these things until after it was too late. I can then blame it mostly on him and pretend that I am the victim. People will feel sorry for me that I am trapped in such a miserable marriage, when I am actually achieving my primary outcome (to be 'in the game')."

There are many marriages like this and one wonders if they serve any good purpose. Usually, both partners have the opportunity to get in touch with their own suppressions, which often act as blocks to the ability to feel love. If both partners are truly ready to clear cumbersome psychological and emotional baggage from their respective pasts and sincerely desire to work with each other, they will probably make great spiritual progress as well as bring about a good marriage.

In dealing with this or any other kind of life complexity, the one indispensable element is the willingness to become truly honest. As long as a person employs manipulative behavior, for instance, there will be no chance of real resolution. All hope of true happiness must wait until all the parties in any relationship are telling the total truth to the best of their ability and sincerely willing to seek happiness and the highest good for all.

More commonly, however, such conscious inner work is too challenging and instead of working through the frightening minefield of his own inner complexity, a person will discard his partner and go off in search of another one to make himself feel loved. Such a person is looking to get love rather than give it. He has not yet reached the stage of evolution where unconditional love is born in his life, for unconditional love would seem to him like robbing the self to give to another.

Saying "unconditional" love is really like saying "wet" water, for if love is conditional, it is not truly love. Unconditional love does not mean loving another *instead* of self. It occurs spontaneously when the self expands sufficiently to include another *as fully as* oneself. This is feeling oneness with another. It is not one person sacrificing himself nobly to defer to another, an act which is more akin to martyrdom. Unconditional love is not something you *do* at all; it is something you *experience*. It is a spontaneous filling up and overflowing with divine ardor. Love such as this is powerfully healing and transforming.

Love is the very opposite of fear. Fear separates and isolates and protects the self to the exclusion of others; regardless of the garb it wears, it is a dark and terrible companion. A frightened person seeks safety from that which (in his perception) is the source of threat. Paradoxically, by so doing he will never know the utter safety that comes from choosing to step into the zone of love and face the fear monster head on.

EXPERIENCING TRUE EMPOWERMENT

A person who has evolved to a place of connection with his soul has grown beyond the need to control anyone else. Instead, he seeks to empower. He will not spend his time and energy in attempts to dominate another person, but will endeavor to achieve dominion over himself. Instead of using power over another, a loving person seeks to empower himself and others.*

LOVE IS PRACTICAL

A discussion of love can become very expansive, but life must be practical also. How do you soar in the ethereal skies of soul-nurturing love and still keep your feet on the ground? What are the key elements for integration of the ethereal and the practical in a balanced, transformed life?

In order to live the transformed life, it is necessary to have made the connection to the soul. In order to live with the soul connected to the body, mind and emotions, it is essential to learn guidelines which will work for you in order to live congruently each day with all the elements of your life. Many mundane elements of life may make better sense following a peak experience, which may come through meditation or rebirthing. Thereafter, you may feel much more inspired to deepen your quest for the inner gold. This is an indication that you have begun the realignment with your own True Self.

If you search out the need beneath any desire, you will find one basic motivation. The predominating goal of life is actually reunion with the soul, which is our own essence. It is this hunger which is the true longing behind all others. When the reunion with spirit finally occurs, the individual involved is always overjoyed and relieved.

---

*"He that ruleth his spirit [is better] than he that taketh a city." Proverbs 16:32

Midway through the week-long intensive workshop at Snow Mountain, one man stated, "If I had known this was a spiritual workshop, I never would have come, but I didn't know that 'spiritual' is what I have been seeking all along because I didn't know that 'spiritual' means 'love.' If I left right now, I would already have received more than I ever dreamed I would get. For the first time in my life, I feel like I am home."

UNDERSTANDING THE TRUE GOAL OF LIFE

Imagine opening a newly-acquired board game, complete with many playing pieces and, although eager to begin playing it with your family, you discover that there are no instructions. You would, most likely, return it to the place of purchase for, without instructions, how would you be able to proceed? How would you know the object of the game? Without a clear understanding of the object of the game, how would you know what comprises success or failure? How could you thus learn to make progress or avoid losing ground? How would you know when the game was over? It would seem absurd just to begin playing without having some answers to these questions. In our lives, however, we actually operate pretty much this way.

Most human beings at this very moment are busily pursuing goals which they adopted without question from someone else. Long before your conscious process of thinking began, a vast amount of programming was already in place. If you wish to truly live and not just exist, you must begin a practice of introspection to determine if the principles which guided your family, and thus your formative, childhood years, are ones in which you sincerely believe. You are here to individuate and live your life from the core of your own truth. Ralph Waldo Emerson once said, "An unexamined life is not worth living."

DISCOVERING YOUR OWN UNIQUENESS

It may be that, as a result of sincere introspection, you will wholeheartedly embrace the same principles you acquired from your family. Only then will you have made them your own. The authenticity of your own belief will now pour real power through your activities, whereas, actions performed out of unquestioned conformity will lack aliveness.

The actions of one who has carved out the mountain of his own maturity to mine the pure gold of the soul become extraordinary actions because they are filled with power from the infinite soul. Such a person realizes that there is a magnificent purpose for the living of a day because *every* action becomes a conduit through which this divine energy flows. Life takes on a dignity and meaning that could hardly be glimpsed before. This is why it is said that a saint is a fully mature person.

AWAKENING STIMULATES MANY QUESTIONS

Sooner or later each person begins awakening to this greater awareness. When that occurs, he begins to ask questions: "What am I doing here? Who am I? Why am I different from others in my family and locale? Is there something wrong with me? Why am I not content to occupy myself the way others seem to do? What am I looking for? Does it even exist? What is this longing inside that keeps nagging at me no matter what? What is this life experience all about anyway?"

For most people, these questions lie somewhere beneath the surface, but for increasing numbers of individuals, they press with growing urgency into conscious awareness. A great, swelling tide of humanity is cresting into consciousness with a hunger and yearning that will be satisfied with nothing less than direct connection with the soul. All over the world, it seems there are many unhappy people, who probably think they know what is wrong in their lives. If it were possible to give each disgruntled person a sheet of paper and ask him to write down the one thing in life that would have to change in order to bring him happiness, the chances are high that either he would not actually be able to identify what is missing or that achieving that goal would not bring him true happiness.

WE ARE ALL SEARCHING FOR SOMETHING

Many people believe that money is the most important thing, yet not only is there unhappiness and discontent among the poor but also among persons of every other economic strata from the middle class to the very rich. Others might rank education as the most important element in a successful life and feel that knowledge and information are the answer to the world's ills. Unhappiness, however, is commonly found not only among those who are illiterate but sometimes it is even more pronounced in those who are trained as physicians, lawyers, psychologists and educators. So, while it is very valuable in developing the potential of a human being, education does not bring happiness. There are barren women who believe that if they could just bear a child, they would be happy and there are those who believe they would be happy if they did not have so many children. People who are unhappily married often believe that getting divorced will make them happy and unmarried people frequently believe that finding a marriage partner will bring them happiness. If the weather is cool, we want it to be warm. If it is hot, we wish for cool weather. Everywhere there is much unhappiness and discontent.

For the most part, people do not seem to observe this phenomenon. They are too busy pursuing goals to notice. Many seek goals of more education, more money, more sex, more freedom, more power, less responsibility, more dependence or more independence. Most people consume their vital years in the quest for their goal, perhaps not realizing that such achievement will not necessarily bring happiness.

I believe that this discontent is universal in the human race as a faculty of self-consciousness. But for what purpose? What is this universal discontent? What are people seeking that keeps them pursuing one goal after another?

UNDERSTANDING HUMAN DISCONTENT

The discontent which is inherent in the unconscious dimensions in all human beings is a nagging hunger which will be satisfied with nothing less than realization of one's own spiritual nature. The unconscious is a far greater portion than the conscious mind and determines what will occur at the conscious level, which is the realm of physical life and the zone we usually consider "real."

The unconscious is really the template level. If you imagine a light shining down through an alphabet stencil, you will see the ABC's as light figures on a paper background. The unconscious dimensions can be compared to that stencil; the paper with the light images on it is like three-dimensional life. (From this viewpoint, it seems amusing that we call the paper dimension the "real" one and call the template level, which is the world unseen by physical eyes, the "unreal.") If you want to make a change in the light images on the paper, you must change the openings. If you remove some of the stencil, larger light images will appear.

How does one enlarge the openings in the stencil of the unconscious? Purification work can be done to begin removing those elements that are creating shadows in your life. If you want more enlightenment, you must begin to work on changing things at the unconscious template level. If you dislike the light images, it will do no good to just get rid of that piece of paper. Any other screen will reflect the same images and, sooner or later, you must become willing to do the work on the unconscious in order to change your life. As you begin such work, you are nearing discovery of the one element in life that will bring you happiness. You are nearing reunion with your own True Self.

LOVING

The language of the soul is a language of love. Not love as a mere word, a concept or a teaching, but love as an active experience which energizes and empowers a person toward true spirituality. This is the essence of all true religion. It is the original God-connection woven into the fabric of humanity when mankind was created.

Love is not an emotion. It is the powerful creative force at work throughout the Universe. The state of joy or bliss that is the soul's nature is a transcendant quality which is beyond all emotion. While it is true that an individual often feels the emotion of happiness in association with love, he also can just as easily experience the emotion of sadness with love. This can easily be understood in the case of grief. When a loved one dies, you feel tremendous grief because of the depth of your love for the deceased. You will not feel the same grief, however, over the death of a casual acquaintance.

In order to give love, you must first be experiencing it actively within yourself. This means that the heart center is open and you are vulnerable and unconditional with your ardor and support of the one you are loving. You fully feel love actively within yourself — within your body and being — and then you pour it out toward the other person. What is actually happening, then, is that you are opening yourself to allow the love of the soul to flow into and through you and out to the other person. Uncontaminated by the taint of ego selfishness, this is the pure love of the divine. As such it is healing, supportive and beneficial to all.

This can be achieved without a word being spoken. As a matter of fact, no words will be needed as your love will be registered in the energy field of the other person, who will feel this love, at least unconsciously. On the other hand, if you use words to tell that person that you love him when you are not actually *feeling* love for him, he may smile in response, but his energy field will register the incongruity or outright untruth of your statement and he usually will, as a consequence, experience an unconscious anxiety. If you are truly feeling and expressing unconditional love, it will always reach its target and result in positive benefit. If you are pretending love for another as a way to achieve some personal outcome, whether it is a trade for affection or manipulation of another for some other selfish purpose, you will find that the results will be less than positive.

While a multitude of rules and laws are required to regulate the behavior of people at lower stages of evolution, they become much less necessary when a person reaches that place where he truly loves with his whole heart. A high level of integrity, commitment to excellence, diligence of purpose and a desire to serve others will be his prevailing traits. St. Augustine observed concisely, "Love — then do what you will." The innate character of such a person will always be higher than would be required by rules or laws.

Mankind, especially in the Occidental cultures, has spent many centuries developing the intellect — to such an extreme that the intellect is honored above all and to the exclusion and denial of the love of the heart. Material values are worshipped so exclusively that many people do not truly believe in real love. Most devote the precious energy of their lives to attempts to have their own physical and social needs met. The resulting boredom, which can hover like a gray fog, is testimony to the fact that the conscious quest for the love of the soul has been abandoned in that individual's life.

Love is what all people are seeking. Ultimately, it is all we want for it is all there is. I am aware that this statement makes little sense to the left-brained, conscious mind, but there is a higher plane of consciousness where it is realized that love is the only thing that is real or lasting. In case you are already thinking that such a state is pretty far out and has little to do with your own life, let us discuss its more practical aspects.

INFORMATION DOES NOT HEAL

If you attended a class on nutrition, you would receive useful data about diet, food combining, vitamin and mineral content, minimum daily amounts recommended for good health and food preparation. When you left the class, your body still would lack nourishment because you only received *information*. In order to nourish the body, food must be consumed and, with that, the body would be nourished with or without information. Because you are, essentially, an energy being, only an energy experience will make any real change in you. These same principles apply regarding spiritual nourishment. In order to grow, heal, rejuvenate and mature, you must actually *experience* love.

EXPERIENCE LEADS TO ENLIGHTENMENT

Religion can, and often does, support the development of psychological and spiritual integration, just as good information about nutrition can lead to better health through balanced diet. Many people get distracted by debate over dogma, however, and fail to notice what is *really* occurring in their lives.

Every great religion or spiritual movement was begun by a great prophet who had an actual numinous experience of enlightenment. For many centuries, however, most of the followers of any of these movements have suffered varying levels of spiritual malnutrition because they received information only and never partook of the actual nourishment which inspired the original prophet. It is now time for mankind to partake of spiritual food and not just listen to lectures *about* it. Just as a newborn's perfect nourishment can only come from suckling at the breasts of the mother in whose body he was formed, an individual can be fully satisfied and nourished only by direct contact with the mother matrix of the soul.

Although religion is often an important part of the maturing process of a healthy individual, it is vitally important to realize, quite regardless of dogma or theology, that the only life-sustaining nourishment comes from the divine. There comes a time in spiritual evolution when the universal human drive for wholeness propels the individual to transcend religious structure for his own experience of direct communion with the divine. Just as a magnificent building is a testimony to the appropriate function of scaffolding during the construction phase, transcendent human experience can be a testimony to the success of religion.

NEW RITUALS ARE NEEDED

The average person in western society has lost touch with his mythological roots. This is particularly true in the United States, with the blending of so many cultures, religions and nationalities. We are sorely in need of positive, effective ways to tap the power latent in the subconscious. This power can be tapped through ritual — group dances, songs, stories, devotionals and myths. As we transcend the boundaries of the separate ideological structures of the past and begin to move to a greater religious and spiritual homogenization, we are sorely in need of new ceremonies. Perhaps we can combine aspects of traditional rituals from many cultures with new rites to serve a more universal community.

ALL PATHS LEAD TO GOD

The urge for reunion with the divinity of the soul is irrepressible. No one religion ever has a monopoly on this quest for it is the natural birthright of a human being to reach this place of enlightenment. Just as you have a relationship to your biological parents which transcends your national citizenship, so all humans have a natural, irrevocable relationship to the divine, which transcends religious affiliation.

Climbers may ascend a mountain in many different ways, but those who reach the top all come together as the paths converge in the unobstructed single light at the summit.

Since the vision of All My Parents in 1985, I feel much more a part of the celebration and loving worship of different cultures, races and religions, whether Hindu, Jewish, Christian, Moslem, Native American, or others. After all, the deathless part of a person is the spirit or energy, which cannot be contained in a limited body. Although a form can be utilized for its expression, spirit will not be constrained. If the form becomes too constricted, the energy leaves. If religious mandates become too structured, the true love of the divine is shut out, for spirit will not be legislated by rules. Once the natural, flowing spiritual aliveness leaves, all that remains is a rigid, lifeless structure.

The world of spirituality is a very individual, inward one. The very most that can be contributed by any authority other than that of your own soul are guidelines which you may or may not choose to follow in order to bring about that internal experience. In the quest for wholeness, you must seek until you find that upward path which truly satisfies your own heart, and apply yourself to it with great loyalty, realizing all the while that other paths lead to the same mountaintop.

An increasing number of individuals are experiencing the light and love of the soul in meditation, in rebirthing experiences and through other sound methods. The quotations from many world religions, shown below, are reminders that this divine energy is natural to all true seekers, regardless of culture or theology. If we are ever to achieve peace on earth and brotherhood among people, we must begin to honor the one light which shines in the multicolored lamps of all humanity.

"God is the sun beaming light everywhere."
Tribal African - AFRICAN RELIGIONS

"The radiance of Buddha shines ceaselessly."
Dhammapada - BUDDHISM

"God is light, and in him is no darkness at all."
I John 1:5 - CHRISTIANITY

"In the lotus of the heart dwells Brahman, the Light of lights."
Mundaka Upanishad - HINDUISM

"Allah is the Light of the heavens and the earth."
Koran - ISLAM

"The Lord is my Light; whom shall I fear?"
Psalms 27:1 - JUDAISM

"The Light of Wakan-Tanka is upon my people."
Song of Kablaya - NATIVE AMERICAN RELIGIONS

"The Light of Divine Amaterasu shines forever."
Kurozumi Munetada - SHINTO

"God, being Truth, is the one Light of all."
Adi Granth - SIKHISM

"Following the Light, the sage takes care of all."
Lao Tsu - TAOISM

The Master sat silently as a group of disciples discussed spirituality and religion. A novice asked, "What is the difference?"

Finally the Master spoke. "Spirituality is like milk," he said, "and religion is like a milk carton, which is valuable to the extent that its contents are nourishing, regardless of the brand or the claims on the label."

Christina Thomas

8

Transformation

You can wake up softly with the touch of a feather
or you can insist on getting hit by a locomotive.
Christina Thomas

A young businessman had a severe drinking problem. He had received signals of transformation in his life: severe financial difficulties and family health problems — what could be called mild "wake-up calls," if he had been able to see them. He was married to a woman he loved dearly and their only child, a 4-year-old girl, had been ill for a while. He travelled on business a great deal, indulged in frequent drinking bouts and stayed away from his family longer than necessary. One day, before he left home on yet another business trip, he spent some time with his little daughter. Weak and pale, she asked him to bring her a special doll. He kissed her and promised to bring it to her the very next day.

While away, he conducted his business but, as he often did, indulged in some drinking. Three days later, he still had not returned home when an urgent message came that the child was gravely ill. He rushed home, reached her bedside and held her close. She looked into his eyes and asked, "Daddy, did you bring my doll?" — then died in his arms. He had completely forgotten her request. He easily could have returned two days earlier but had not once remembered his promise to her. He plummeted into inconsolable grief.

Years later he related the lesson he had learned: "I could have awakened with the touch of a feather for, when I look back with eyes that can see, I realize that there had been signals which were like mild wake-up calls. I ignored those signals. When my little girl died in my arms, it was like being hit by a locomotive. After that, it was as though scales had been ripped off my eyes and, for the first time, I could see what really mattered in my life."

THE SHIFT TO INTERNAL POWER

Transformation beyond self-conscious life means that you must begin transcending the limited identity with the visible world and become acquainted with the vast world of the unseen. Such transcendance encompasses the conscious yielding to energies coming from higher spiritual dimensions which communicate with the physical body. In most people, the conscious mind is disconnected from these higher energies and life is, therefore, focused in this mundane way to the exclusion of the higher. The challenge, then, is to bring the conscious mind into alignment with these higher energies by yielding to the direction of the soul. Only when this occurs are you completely available to transcendance.

When the ego is brought into obedience as the servant of the soul, there is a letting go of reliance on the power of the external world and a commencement of trust in the inner. Many people are unacquainted with their own feelings and rely almost entirely on outer power. When the inner divinity decrees that awakening time has arrived, one can choose to surrender or resist. If resistance is the choice, the wake-up call may become louder and louder, until the exterior structures completely collapse. Sometimes this is in the form of cancer or other health breakdown, or financial failure, relationship failure or other disaster. Once such a breakdown occurs, there is no way to put things back the way they were and the looming, unavoidable transformation occurs.

The phenomenon of labor in pregnancy is an example of the process of transformation. Pregnancy is relatively peaceful for nine months, but when the time of birth nears, the onset of labor signals that the peaceful status quo is breaking down. Relatively mild initial contractions begin to propel the baby's head lower into the birth canal. They become more frequent and much stronger as labor progresses, culminating in the birth of a healthy child. If you had no knowledge of how this natural process works, you might think of labor as some terrible, unwarranted trauma. This is *exactly* the way many people respond to transformation in their own lives. Not understanding that birth to a higher consciousness is imminent, they resist the process as some awful accident. When you can recognize the signals of transformation in your own life and beome willing to surrender, life's contractions will not necessarily be easy, but they will be easier than if you resist.

THE STAGES OF TRANSFORMATION

Friedrich Nietzsche said that the process of human transformation has three stages: When a person is young, he is like a camel who gets down on its knees and says, "Put a load on me." When the camel is sufficiently burdened, he turns into a lion and runs out into the desert alone. Eventually the lion must find and slay the "Thou Shalt" dragon. (On every scale of this dragon is written, "Thou shalt" or "Thou shalt not.") Once this dragon is slain, the lion becomes a little child walking in its own light, like a wheel rolling out of its own center.

In this metaphor, "putting a load on the camel" is comparable to the process of taking on the values of family, culture, religion and society at large,* which are all arbitrary, regardless of how sacrosanct and inarbitrary they are held out to be. It is true that a structure is necessary for healthy development, but the *content* of that structure will differ from one culture to another. For example, if a child is born in China of Chinese parents, his ideology will be different from that of a child born to Caucasians in the United States. Each child receives a different set of beliefs and each set forms the scaffolding to construct the building of that young life.

When the camel is sufficiently loaded, (when the young person is sufficiently enculturated), it "runs out into the desert, alone, and turns into a lion." This means that the young person must leave the protective environment of childhood home (at least psychologically) and, being strong like the lion, go out into the world on his own. Unless and until the ego structure of a person is sufficiently strong,** he

---

*"It is good for a man that he bear the yoke in his youth." Lamentations 3:27

**A *strong* ego is different than a *big* ego. A big ego is weak and inflated like a balloon; it has a chip on each shoulder and will as easily take offense as inflict it. It seeks to be right above all. A strong ego, in contrast, is sufficiently disciplined to withstand difficulty without collapsing under stress. In any endeavor, a person must have ego strength to make worthwhile progress.

cannot leave his childhood and go alone into the world. For the lion will be only as strong as the camel was burdened.

Once the strong lion goes out into the desert alone, he must find and slay the "Thou Shalt" dragon. This dragon is a symbol for all the rules and values received from sources external to the child, which are set in place during the formative years. It must be killed not because these precepts are defective in any way, but because they have true power in the individual life only after this process. This means that the person *must* individuate each value for himself, sorting out whether or not it has meaning for him, if he is to live authentically.

Once this process is complete, the "Thou Shalt" dragon is dead. The values loaded onto him in the enculturation process in childhood have now been examined one by one and he has retained only those which are authentically true for him. Even if a particular value is retained, once it is individuated it no longer belongs to the realm of external power. The person then becomes like the little child walking in his own light.* Now fully mature and individuated, he becomes childlike, able to responsibly perform his duties in the world and retain all the spontaneity, delight and wonder of a child. Embodying all of the assets of maturity with none of the shortcomings, he has come full circle and is able to maintain his balance regardless of outward circumstances.

---

*The disciples of Jesus asked, "Who is the greatest in the kingdom of heaven?" (Matthew 18:1) This scripture continues, "And Jesus called a little child unto him, and set him in the midst of them and said, Verily I say unto you, Except ye ... become as little children, ye shall not enter into the kingdom of heaven." (Matthew 18:2, 3).

Nietzsche's further comparison that he is like "a wheel rolling out of its own center" means that wherever he goes, he will be "centered" and able to make congruent decisions and choices for himself, whether or not others agree with those decisions or choices. In summation, such a person knows where he is going in life because he has achieved a sufficient degree of oneness within himself.

METAMORPHOSIS

You are not going to experience transformation in some mild, tea-party kind of way. Transformation, though blissful and valuable, is not an easy undertaking. You will not succeed in freeing yourself of ego domination by listening to some nice subliminal tapes while you fall asleep. You must go against your old, instinctual patterns in order to transform into the divine person. Carl Jung referred to this as "opus contra naturam" (work against nature). As the term implies, you must forsake what is natural to the self-conscious way of life in order to begin your metamorphosis into a superconscious being. This process is a huge transition.

All the cycles of our birth, growth, death and rebirth herald big changes and a letting go of the way things have been in order to allow the new way that life will be. As uncomfortable as change is and as much as we resist it in attempts to preserve the status quo, we must recognize that life itself is a process of continual change. The only constant in the universe is change. To resist change is to resist life. When labor is complete, the baby who fails to emerge from the womb will die. To embrace change, therefore, is to embrace new life.

Once a person truly begins awakening and becoming more spiritually conscious, nothing ever again happens by accident, if ever it did. When difficulties come, the sincere person will not seek ways that help his former small self to survive. Instead, he will turn to those who encourage him to risk even more, knowing that as he willingly endures and even embraces the suffering, he is passing through it the quickest way possible.

SURRENDERING TO PURIFICATION

The goal is not to reach a place of safety where you will be immune to difficulties. Quite the contrary, by realizing that you are refining the pure gold of the soul in the fires of purification, you must finally become willing to remain vulnerable to assaults and perturbations — passing through the refiner's fire to reach that which has always awaited you beyond the identification with a reality that is limited.

It is as though each of us has a golden shore of peace and love, but between you and your golden shore lies a swamp full of alligators. In order to reach the other side, you must head into the murky swamp, indeed you must be willing to drink every dirty drop and face every one of those alligators, willing even to die rather than postpone your quest any longer. Virtually all that would have to happen to have heaven on earth, according to Dr. Carl Jung, would be for each person to own his own shadow, the shadow being all those qualities which have been judged, disowned and subsequently projected out onto someone or something else.

As long as elements of the shadow remain suppressed and disowned by you, these elements will seem like monsters. Your *willingness* to go through this process of owning your own shadow to face whatever life brings, then, becomes a lifeboat that takes you to your golden shore. Only then will you realize that the whole swamp and all those terrifying monsters were never real in the first place, but were only illusion. As you confront, instead of avoid, whatever terror lurks inside and continue to breathe while observing your own feelings (without blaming them on yourself or anyone else), you empty yourself of old emotional and psychological baggage which you probably have carried for a long time.

Although this period of emptiness is temporary, it is nonetheless essential to endure it, for only if you can allow yourself to be empty, can you ever be filled. Great strength is required to hold the tension of these powerful, paradoxical energies, but this is the direct way in which you will achieve great soul growth.

A Samurai sword in the making is passed through the fire more than a hundred times, a process which purifies every piece of dross and leaves its steel so hard that it can cut through anything. In a similar way, only as you expose your very being over and over again to the illusory inner monsters, can that part of you which is indestructible be born from within.

In order to unleash the passion and power which will give your life the meaning you fervently desire, you must be courageous enough to honestly face your life, experiencing it all, the easy and the difficult. In this way you can accept and even welcome the fear which arises from your own unconscious. This process is very different from attempts to keep this fear suppressed and thereby pretend a little longer that it does not exist.

When you surrender to the worst that terror threatens you with, you soon pierce through a veil of illusion that seemed very real before. Disrobed and exposed for the imposter that it is, the fear finally ceases its terrorism. Stripped of all intimidation, it now becomes your ally. The enormous energy on which this parasite has been feeding is released at last to reintegrate into your own wholeness of being.

Only as you risk venturing into this territory can that which is indestructible arise from the depths of your innermost self. Thus you will build a strong, reliable, finely-tuned instrument into which divine energy will flow and through which it will carry out its ecstatic, loving plan. Your life will then literally become a temple filled with love and wisdom and the full realization will dawn upon you that you essentially are powerful, divine and limitless.

I existed long before this lifetime -
not the small "i"
but the I that is a part of
the energy that permeates all of Universe.
I wear a finite body
with a limited personality,
but my True Self
is part of the energy of all.
There is no need to seek an intermediary
to contact the infinite source,
for I can contact it
directly now.
Requiring another to interpret for me
is to allow my infinite ability
to lay dormant.
Through the instrument
of my attunement
and receptivity,
Light is directed to me
as intuitive knowing.
There is no beginning nor end - no place to go.
My only real task is a joyful one:
to stay in tune with the soul.

9

Purpose

*When your personal goals align with your
soul's mighty purpose, a sense of peace, power
and passion will infuse the days of your life.*
Christina Thomas

The ultimate purpose of human life is to achieve conscious reunion with the love of the divine. This is what your soul wants for you and what it relentlessly works to bring about in a variety of ways. Regardless of the events in your personal life, it is always working to reunite your conscious mind, your personality and your physical body with its energy.

At the moment of your conception, when this divine activating element joined that first fertilized cell and began the process of cell division and formation of your little baby body, your spirit was clearly aware of its purpose for this incarnation. Whether or not you are aware of it, this reuniting is the transpersonal purpose of your life as a human being. In response to the yearning which is set up by this dynamic deep within the unconscious, every human being is seeking reconnection with this love and will be satisfied with nothing less.

There is much variety in the many ways the soul goes about creating opportunities for the movement toward this reunion. Certainly, it is not interested in the mundane details of everyday life, although these concerns may seem very important to an individual. Ultimately, these are all temporary and illusory, and the soul is concerned only with the eternal. Earth life is a school, however, and these human dramas are important in that they provide the elements which function as catalysts for the opening up of conscious awareness to divine love. The soul often utilizes the events of life to maneuver us into position so we will yield to spirit when the time comes.

I recently watched a toddler as he played with some alphabet building blocks. He happily busied himself, secure in the knowledge that his mother was nearby. Suddenly, the little house he was building came crashing down, the blocks scattering in colorful disarray. He began wailing and mama came running to attend to him. Seeing that there was nothing to be concerned about, she smiled, gathered him into her arms and held him close to her, while big crocodile tears ran down his little cheeks. His catastrophe over, mother placed him back on the floor to play again and went on about her business. As disastrous as the collapse of his little structure was to him, his parent was unmoved, being peacefully aware that it was of no consequence. She knows that while he is playing and struggling with all his infantile disasters, his little teeth are forming, his bones are growing, he is steadily developing small and large-motor coordination, and so forth - - all the elements truly important in his life are unaffected by his upset. The toddler can be all caught up in his playthings today and this creates no interference in the vitally important growth which is taking place within him.

It often seems to me that the soul functions the same way. God, perhaps as Divine Mother and through the intermediary of the soul, does not get caught up in the little failures or successes of our everyday lives, which we often think are of such consequence, for the soul knows that we are steadily growing toward the realization of our own divinity, regardless of our lack of awareness that this is taking place.

When the soul wants you to wake up and stop being preoccupied with a favorite plaything, it sometimes will cause a structure to collapse. You may howl with pain when this happens in your life, for these wake-up calls are often shocking and painful, but if you wind up in Divine Mother's arms, the purpose will have been well served and you will eventually realize it yourself.

TRUSTING THE SOUL

In whatever external form you place your trust other than the inner soul connection, you doom that construct to collapse eventually so that you will be motivated to find your way back home. If you identify yourself through your husband or wife, lover or child, you may set up an unconscious requirement for that person to leave you, so that you may gradually approach the realization of your true identity. Often such a person will begin to feel a strong urge to walk out, without realizing why he feels this way. He may even consciously desire to stay with you and yet make efforts to leave because of your inappropriate grasping for safety in the relationship.

If your trust in life is tied up with prestige and achievement, you may only begin to listen to the soul's promptings with the advent of disgrace and failure. If you think that your safety lies in money, this may presage a financial collapse. In short, placing your trust in external power requires that power, eventually, to collapse. As you sift through the debris of such a wreckage, it is possible to discover eternal values which are like pure gold compared to the debris you have just wept over and lost. Try as you may to set life up nicely and then keep it that way, the soul is ever working to shake you out of the lethargy of a stagnant status quo so you can experience the constantly changing yet ever peaceful, true life of the soul.

LOVING YOUR WORK

At the same time, the divine plan for reunion with the soul is evolution through free choice. God never takes away your free will, so you have latitude within which to choose how you will express yourself in life. As you experiment to determine where your likes, dislikes and natural abilities lead you, you will uncover a sense of purpose through which you will find meaning and happiness. When you engage in activities that make you feel happy, you reap a wonderful reward from each moment. This happiness is a signal that you are feeling at least a trickle of the soul's love. You may find that you delight in hands-on work with colors and shapes and may choose to express this interest by being an artist, working with fabrics, studying architecture or designing interiors. If you find yourself completely engrossed in the details of your work and the hours fly by, you are probably on the right track. When you spend your time this way, the love of the soul easily flows through you to create excellent results, whether you are working on a temporary job, engaging in a chosen profession or enjoying a favorite hobby.

If, however, you dread the very thought of getting up in the morning, you can be sure that either your day-to-day activity does not serve the purpose for which your soul came into your present physical body, or there is a lesson inherent in this situation which your soul wants you to learn.

Recently I counseled a schoolteacher who complained at length about her work. She expressed much dissatisfaction with her job and I finally asked her, "How long are you going to work at something you dislike so much? Why not give yourself permission to do some other work that might make you happier?"

"Oh, it isn't really so bad," she responded. "I am glad I got my degree to work in this field. This is what I really want to do. It's just that there are some parts of it I don't like."

Sensing that she was hiding from her true feelings, I asked, "What if you won the ten-million-dollar lottery? Would you keep your job?"

"Of course not!" she retorted emphatically, confirming my suspicion. "I would never teach school another day in my life!"

"Then this is not what your soul wants to do," I said quietly. "When you do work you love, you do not engage in it *primarily* because of the income, even though you may earn your living from it." I shared with her my feelings about my own work: "Even if I needed no additional funds, I would still do the work I am already doing because I truly love it. When I am working on a book, for instance, I often awaken spontaneously in the wee hours of the morning and spend quiet, uninterrupted time writing. I love my work so much that I genuinely look forward to the experience of it. Each moment contains its own reward."

When your daily activity aligns with the soul's (transpersonal) purpose, this kind of thrilling satisfaction results, and you will be happy. In direct proportion to this attunement you will feel the peace of the soul. You will be happy if you are fulfilling the soul's purpose. You will feel restless and unhappy if you are not.

HAPPINESS NOT DEPENDENT ON CIRCUMSTANCES

The joy and satisfaction that come from attunement with the soul do not disappear when outer circumstances become painful. This is "dual consciousness," wherein a person is aware of events in the outer world that may be tragic, painful or frightening (on the darker side) or intense, thrilling and ecstatic (on the joyful side), but the inner world remains peaceful. Many women experience this with the birth of a child. Although the body may be caught up in terrifically intense and painful contractions during labor and birth, the whole process may be an experience of ecstatic union so blissful that it defies description. As I mentioned earlier, this was my experience when my daughter was born.

It is fairly easy to understand this concept as it applies to childbirth, which, though challenging, is a happy occasion. Much more of a stretch is required to comprehend that circumstances lacking any happy element can also be the catalyst which pierces the membrane of ego isolation and allows one to feel the soul's love.

I gained an acute awareness of this psycho-spiritual dynamic as a result of direct experience with my husband's sudden illness. As I moved through those first days filled with shock and anguish, the hot grief which I felt more or less continuously seemed to widen the portal to the inner sanctuary. A spiritual love, more intense than any in my life, permeated my being and my whole body felt super-oxygenated, tingling with electrical energy. In these circumstances, the pain which I felt was piercing, but at the same time I was shielded by a preternatural divine ardor which enveloped me in its protective aura. I was in sacred space.

Enduring this ordeal, I struggled to find some meaning or resolution. Alas, no quick resolution came and life took its time to reveal any meaning. I have come to believe that the painful inner writhing stimulated by the intense urge to resolve such a painful dilemma is a necessary part of the process and ultimately fuels the spiritual breakthrough which is sure to come if the tension between pain and relief can be held. At such a time, it is actually a great blessing that no quick relief comes, for enduring the suffering can lead to a far higher place. T. S. Eliot eloquently expressed this necessary surrender to the soul's timing as follows:

"I said to my soul: 'Be still and wait without hope,
for hope would be hope for the wrong thing. Wait
without love for love would be love of the wrong
thing. There is yet faith, but the faith and the hope
and the love are all in the waiting. And do not think,
for you are not ready for thought. So the darkness
shall be the light and the stillness the dancing.'"

This is beautifully stated and it might seem even clearer to
paraphrase this as, *"My soul said to me . . ."* For it is the soul
which knows the wisdom and when you can hear its whis-
pers you are open to receiving that wisdom and can endure
the stillness, the waiting and the darkness. When the time
comes, you will emerge into a light greater than you could
have endured before.

FINDING YOUR PURPOSE

When you awaken to the memory of your true identity and
shake off residual spiritual amnesia, you will feel a deeper
sense of purpose than ever before. Life seems meaningless to
one who is disconnected from the soul, and his attempts to
create false meaning out of the material values of this world
invariably result in disappointment. Such a person is never
satisfied because, intrinsically, he is a *spiritual* being and
material values can *never* satisfy spirit.

When you open the door to your soul and allow its love to
transform your body, mind and personality, that energy
flows through you to other people and into everything you

do. When you prepare a meal, the love of the soul will permeate the food and provide strength and regeneration for those blessed by its nourishment. When you create a painting, the soul's aliveness will splash onto the canvas and complete its meaning again and again in the receptive eyes of each beholder. When you write a book, the intelligence of the soul will move between the lines, stimulating the latent awareness and perfection in the reader. When you conduct your business, the wisdom and intuition of the soul will lead to greater efficiency and effectiveness than the conscious mind, alone, could possibly arrange and the increased financial gain which frequently accompanies this will be a fortunate by-product. In all these circumstances, your presence and interaction will benefit others even without a word being spoken and your relationships with others will become alive, sincere, authentic and full of meaning.

RESOURCE = RETURN (RE) TO THE SOURCE

Lacking the connection to the power of the soul is like operating a piece of electrical equipment solely from a battery. Eventually this will exhaust the energy reserve in the battery and the equipment will cease to work. But connect the equipment directly to the house current via a wall outlet and it will operate continuously at full power. When a person accepts the premise that he must rely solely on the finite power of the conscious mind to manage all of life, he, understandably, has constant concern over the amount of reserve left in the body/mind battery. This false limitation leads to great fear: fear of abandonment, fear of running out of money and fear of living without love. *Without questioning the false belief itself*, most people respond to this fear by devoting their entire lives to avoiding the negative results they fear, but the only effective remedy for this miserable state is to connect directly to the ongoing supply of the infinite source. No longer need there be concern for exhausting the remaining reserve, for this source is unlimited.

As a matter of fact, it is the use of energy which calls for more. This is a natural principle of life. Every nursing mother knows that when her baby sucks the milk from her breasts, the body automatically responds by replacing the supply. Production ceases, however, when the breasts are already full. It is the process of consuming which calls for more milk. This principle works the same way with other forms of energy. As it is used, more is provided. The fortunate person who experiences such abundance becomes free to focus on the creativity and power which pours through as an unlimited supply in his life.

How would it change the next hour of your life if you imagined that you were directly connected to a loving God and could totally trust that all your needs were being met perfectly? Think about this right now. Would that not mean that you could take a deep breath and relax? Wouldn't it mean that you need have no anxious concern for your own welfare and, therefore, could enjoy just being in the present moment the way you did when you were a little child? Take this exercise to heart and experience the miracles that can come out of it. A German saying translates as: "Never go to a second thing first." As you do this exercise, you may become clearer about your priorities. When you begin to attune to the power within, you will realize that the first priority is to be connected to your soul and thus open yourself to the direct infusion of its energy into your life.

10

Attitudes of Attunement

"When you have the right attitude, every circumstance becomes a source of spiritual benefit and transformation. Right attitude activates the power of divinity in your life."

Christina Thomas

Of all the tools available with which to change your life, adopting right attitude is one of the most effective. While an entire volume could be devoted to this important category, included here are a few which can work like magic to transform your life.

REVERENCE

Reverence is deeply honoring all of life. It is an awareness that God is in everyone and everything. Reverence goes way beyond respect, which contains an element of judgment. You respect someone if he measures up to *your* standards. If you have reverence for all life, however, even though you may lack respect for a person's behavior, you will not mistreat him. You will honor his essence, quite regardless of his behavior. This reverence in the very face of unacceptable behavior is a powerful, transformative attitude.

Your happiness in life is directly linked to how much reverence you have — reverence for life, for others, for all creatures and even for circumstances. Human beings are happiest when their behavior is unselfconscious, reverent and loving and are least happy when it is self-righteous and judgmental.

You become stuck when you judge anything or anyone. As a matter of fact, if you judge anything, you are judging yourself and by doing so, you will lose some of your sense of freedom. If someone is judging you, you will also find that nothing said will hurt you unless some part of you thinks it is true. When you judge a person, for instance, you pay attention to *how* he uses or qualifies the energy moving through him and you make judgments about that *how*, instead of remembering that the energy itself is neutral. The fact that he is misusing it *at this time* does not mean that he will continue to misuse it.

When Mary Magdalene was about to be stoned for committing adultery, she certainly knew that her behavior had been in violation of Jewish law. That information did nothing to change her. It was the pure, unconditional love offered by the Christ which ignited her transformation. Cleansed and healed of the psychological and emotional wounds which had led her to the insanity of prostitution, she embarked on a new life.

As you refrain from judging and look beyond another person's behavior to behold the vision of his essential divinity, you actually help him claim the higher identity when he is ready. Your love, your light, your vision and your positive thoughts create a powerful vortex of light and energy around that person, making it easier for him to transform when the time is ripe. When you behave in such a positive manner, it benefits not only the other person, but moves you quickly along your journey, also, for the reverence you have for others is directly linked to the spiritual strength you build within yourself. An ego-shackled, self-centered person suffers from feelings of pitiful unworthiness, for instance, and seems to fear that if he acknowledges the excellence of another, it somehow detracts from himself. Attempts to compensate for such low self-esteem with a show of arrogance and self-importance usually alienate others and further reinforce his self-imposed prison, whereas an attitude of reverence for his fellow man could begin to liberate him. Sometimes when I observe such desperate behavior, I remember the following quotation, which recognizes this tie between reverence and spiritual stamina:

> "He who cannot bow his knee in reverence to anyone
> will at last be unable to bear the weight of his own self."
>   Author Unknown

PREFERENCE OR ATTACHMENT?

Once a person begins awakening, he will benefit by better understanding the subject of attachment, which is frequently somewhat confusing. It is not uncommon to wonder how it is possible to be truly involved in life and yet not be attached to a chosen outcome. This reminds me of a humorous exchange that occurred as an expectant father waited at the hospital for news of the birth of his first child. The anxious young man sprang out of his seat as a delivery room nurse burst through the door and asked, "Sir, did you want a boy or a girl?"

"A girl," he replied, breathless with anticipation.

"Well," she answered, "you have a little boy."

"Oh, good!" the young father beamed. "That was my second choice!"

This brief exchange illustrates a formula which can work like magic. The new father wanted a girl but was not *attached* to having a girl. Instead of wanting a girl and not wanting a boy, a game in which he could either win or lose, he had a different perspective: "My first choice is a girl and my second choice is a boy. I will take whatever God gives." This is an approach where no one loses.

This seems pretty clear but the subject of attachment can still be confusing. People sometimes say, for instance, "I have strong desires for the fulfillment of certain needs and goals in my life. How can I not be attached?" Let us look further.

A person plants a garden and tends it dutifully with skill and love, always with the desire for an abundant crop at harvestime. A flood comes and washes away the precious plants. He feels terrible and wonders why it happened to him. He may feel hopeless and reluctant to start all over again. The result he wanted was to reap the food at harvest. He was attached to that outcome and has lost his happiness along with his crop.

Let us look at the same garden planted by a spiritual person, who tends it just as dutifully, knowing that this is his work. When the flood washes away the crop, although he may feel some temporary disappointment, he will plant the garden again, for he realizes that the result is up to God and it is enough for him to do the work at hand from day to day. Yes, this spiritual person *prefers* to reap a good crop but is not *attached* to it, for he reaps his true reward in each moment that he engages in work he loves.

This is an important distinction. Attachment closes up your connection to the joy and power of the soul and can become addictive. If you are deprived of something you are attached to, you feel a sense of loss, as if you are not complete without it. Not only will you feel unhappy, but you will be unable to function as well. In short, you lose your *center*. This is true whether the addiction is for a substance, a person, a certain kind of food or a particular outcome to a situation. The attachment or addiction has power over you.

On the other hand, if you have only a preference for something, you will be able to remain poised and calm whether or not you receive it. You may experience some disappointment but it will not seriously affect your state of mind, and you will be able to enjoy your second choice or something else.

A social worker shared a deep concern. She said, "I had to stop working in my profession because I felt so burned out with all the problems of the people I was trying to help. No matter how hard I worked or how much I cared, when all was said and done, those poor, needy people were still poor and needy. I began to feel that it was impossible to accomplish anything and felt hopeless and needy myself. I had to find a different kind of job."

This young woman was attached to making certain changes in the lives of the people she served. While this is understandable, it was clearly not within her power to bring about all those changes in the ways she desired. Because she measured the success of her efforts by the results achieved in the world around her, she felt like a failure even though she had done her very best.

I thought about Mother Teresa of Calcutta, who knows that it is her work to move among the poorest of the poor and help whomever she meets from moment to moment. On occasion, people have asked her, "What good does it do if you find someone and take care of him and he dies that same day? What are you *really* accomplishing here?" She always answers with the same powerful clarity, "If that person feels the love of Christ even *once* in his life, then I have served well. My job is to love."

So, while Mother Teresa and those of her order assuredly prefer that those they serve become healthy and strong, they are not attached to that outcome. She knows that when she dies, Calcutta and many other places in the world will still be peopled with many thousands who are suffering disease and poverty. The ego mind would measure Mother Teresa's effectiveness by counting the number of people helped *in its opinion*. But her mission is being fulfilled and the joy and enthusiasm is full and complete for her and her helpers for they understand that they are like gardeners tilling the soil and the harvest is God's business.

Having preferences instead of attachments leaves you squarely in the driver's seat of your life. You give none of your power away to the object you desire. You prefer it, but you feel complete with or without it. When you begin practicing and living with this principle, you will feel comfortable much more of the time.

LETTING EVERYTHING BE OKAY

There always seem to be situations in life that one is unwilling to allow. The usual response is resistance, which, of course, does not remedy the unacceptable situation. Since you have no choice but to deal with some unpleasant occurrences, practical ways to respond effectively are needed.

My discovery of the power of yielding to a painful situation rather than resisting it occurred after my husband was stricken in 1978. Medical personnel did not limit me to the usual five minutes visitation per hour while he was comatose and in the Intensive Care Unit. Instead I was allowed to stand next to his bed day after day and had many silent hours in which a number of deep realizations were revealed from within.

Quite obviously, I did not have the power to restore him to vigorous health so that our family life could go on as before. I was literally writhing with inner anguish over this tragedy and found myself wondering if I had attracted it by my efforts to speed up the balancing out of my karma. I had always eagerly sought spiritual growth, feeling that it could not come too quickly. Suddenly, for the first time in my life,

I began to contemplate whether or not I wanted to ask God to back off a bit and allow me to evolve a little more slowly. (This thought came as my mind darted from point to point as a way to figure out why this calamity had occurred and whether there was anything I could have done to prevent it. If you have ever experienced such a tragic loss, you most likely found the conscious mind going a little crazy, desperately thrashing about and seeming out of control.)

As I reflected on the possibility of slowing down, I realized that this was inappropriate. In that moment, standing in the Intensive Care Unit, I surrendered to the changes in our lives and found the prayer that would work for me: "Dear God, I never again want to endure such an experience. Please help me to learn whatever lessons I need to play my role well in this disastrous drama and be able to serve my husband and my child sweetly."

Although I was unaware at the time how much strength would come from this shift in attitude, I thus had found a way to accept the adversity. In no way does this mean that I liked the situation or ceased to struggle with it. What I realized clearly, however, was that there was vitally important work and service for me in the present moment. I had to become both mother and father for our little girl, for instance, and there were many details to manage as I undertook the burden of single-handedly running the family business. In addition, it was important to be at the hospital with Bill every day. If my energy was caught in resisting the situation, I could not serve effectively. I allowed myself to feel the grief as it came up from moment to moment, but I continuously turned to God with the pain, asking for help in handling it. I did not have control over the circumstance, but I could control my response to it.

In order to get through those heartbreaking days, I inwardly cried out to God a countless number of times. When the anguish seemed too great to bear and I felt unable to endure a whole hour, I would traverse only the next minute, going within again and again. The willingness to do this - to go to God with everything - became the source of greatest strength for me.

A momentous revelation comes when you realize that the Universe and everything in it are already perfect, regardless of your perception of them. Although you may not believe this yet, you can test it in the laboratory of your own life by following the exercise below. While it is not difficult, it may take time to master the technique. Certainly, it is well worth the practice.

Exercise:

Look around at something in your life that you resist and begin letting it be okay just as it is. It is fine to prefer that it change but do not make it wrong as it currently exists. Notice that even the most painful, disastrous events that can happen to a human being eventually become okay. A hundred years ago there were human beings on this planet who had problems similar to or worse than yours and, most likely, they believed that those problems were extremely serious. But where are those people today? Those souls which have already reincarnated are inhabiting newer bodies and utilizing other challenges to continue learning needed lessons. So even if you have to go in fantasy to a time one hundred years from now in order to be able to let everything be okay, it is helpful to find a way to do it.

Here is another tactic that works when all else fails: If you encounter something that you just cannot accept as it is, then take one step back and let it be okay that you cannot accept it as it is. And if that does not work, then usually the next step will: Let it be okay that you cannot even find it within yourself to accept everything.

Please do not decide with your mind whether or not this exercise works, for you will only get the benefit from it when you actually apply it to a real-life situation. Then you can either discard it as a useless notion or you will have discovered a valuable new self-empowerment tool. Work with your mind to allow the release of energy and creativity that comes from letting everything be okay. In order to have peace in your life, you must find a way to accept whatever circumstances life presents.

ASKING FOR HELP

The spiritual path is wonderfully rewarding but it is not easy. If you attempt to walk alone, it becomes impossible. The willingness to call out for help is indispensable. Adopting this attitude will build great strength and true humility in your life, for it is a constant reminder that God is the doer and your role is only to be in attunement with the Divine will. With such surrender to the soul's direction, you will be able to place your foot in the next appropriate step, even when you cannot see where the road is leading. This frees you from anxious preoccupation with any unknown future turn of events, allowing you to perform optimally in the present moment. A long chain of such well-lived present moments creates a life which is a glowing testimony to the power of the soul expressing through the vehicle of a spiritually awakened human being.

THE NAUGHTY BABY

A toddler in his playpen awakens from a nap and cries for his mother, who sends a nuresemaid with a bottle. The baby rejects the bottle and cries louder. Mother sends his nanny with a toy, which he also refuses. His incessant wailing threatens to shatter the eardrums of everyone in the house. Then mother, herself, puts down her other work and comes to him. He reaches out to her, nestles into her bosom and ceases his crying, a happy smile radiating out from his flushed little face.

When you become like the naughty baby and will be satisfied with nothing less than the supreme gift of God's direct embrace, your heart's desire will be close at hand. For countless lifetimes, we chase after many distracting playthings, whether material possessions, political power or human relationships, seeking fulfillment from these achievements and acquisitions to the neglect of the spirit. When we finally tire of the pursuit of other goals, having experienced enough, we are nearing the ultimate goal.

It is said that when one calls out for God as intently as a drowning man gasps for air, then God will come. A passage from the Bhagavad Gita emphasizes this attitude of relying on the Divine in every instant, even as you participate in each human drama.

> "Who sees Me everywhere
> Who sees all in Me
> For him I am not lost
> Nor is he lost for Me."

11

A New Paradigm

"...Ye are gods and all of you are children of the most High."

Psalms 82:6

Look up at the ceiling of the Sistine Chapel and behold one of the greatest artistic masterpieces on earth. Michaelangelo's passionate rendering of man's creation touches such depths that all attempts at description are inadequate. Imagine how much would be lost if only a minute section of this vast painting were enclosed in a small frame and the rest obliterated. The small portion included within the limited confines would convey nothing of meaning and would fall far short of representing the original majestic rendering.

Similarly, current models of theology, sociology and psychology attempt to enclose a vast image in a tiny frame. Conventional thought in the western world discusses only the mind, accepting only that which can be understood mentally. The mind is finite, however, and only begins to form after the almighty soul commences preparation of the physical body and the concomitant, all-important brain and spinal centers. These supersensitive cerebro-spinal centers link the vehicle of the physical body to its home of spirit through interchanges of light or energy.

The mind is intended to serve as an instrument for the light or energy from the soul, but lacking an open connection and conscious willingness to allow spirit's flow, it is as pitifully unable to move wisely in life's waters as a sailboat without a crew. Just as a computer does not have the capacity to understand or evaluate the engineer who designed it, the finite mind is incapable of assessing the infinite. A human being functioning without the conscious link to the soul is like a billionaire who is suffering from lack of money because his wealth is tied up in untapped certificates of deposit.

Life's eternal verities - whether called God, soul, love or any other name - are infinite and, therefore, beyond the mind. When we choose to accept only that which the mind can grasp, we severely limit our scope. We must enlarge our view if we are to function wisely and claim our birthright as joyful, liberated children of divinity. When the bigger picture is seen, whole chunks that seemed mysterious before begin to move clearly into focus, fall into place and make practical sense. A new paradigm is coming into being, based on the ancient truth that a human being is a god in the making.

If our planetary family is to be healed of its many ills, we human beings must begin awakening to the underlying truth about ourselves. Theology has long taught that human beings are divine offspring, but there has been so little individual direct experience of this phenomenon that humanity as a whole continues to suffer in ignorance of its true origin. In order to learn to relate to each other peacefully -

which we must do if this race of people is to survive - we must begin to heal our misconceptions and accomodate a world-wide healing. No longer can we afford to rely solely on a small contingent of clerics to interpret the world of spirit for us. We must also begin to trust our inner knowing and relate directly to the divine, taking responsibility for our own connection with spirit. Regardless of your theology, if you are to tap the unlimited potential of your infinite beingness, you must have a direct, personal relationship with the soul.

THE SOUL'S ENTRY INTO HUMAN FORM

At the moment of human conception, souls ready for re-embodiment and waiting in the astral dimension become aware of the opportunity for reincarnating. There are many more souls waiting for bodies than there are bodies available. Among souls of ordinary spiritual evolution, there is a great rushing and scrambling to seize the immediate opportunity. There is, of course, always enough of a correspondence between any of these souls and the potential new family for the incoming soul to learn needed life lessons. Earth life is a school and an incarnation could be seen as a semester. There are a great number of subjects which must be studied and mastered before promotion to the next grade and eventual graduation.

In the case of a new family where even one of the parents has any true spiritual advancement, however, there is no scrambling among souls waiting to reincarnate, for the blessing of being born to such a couple is assigned to a soul who has earned this privileged spot through its own conscious, spiritual effort in a past lifetime. Being nurtured by this parent or family, he will naturally be propelled to make more spiritual progress.

All the soul cares about is spiritual growth. It does not care whether a lifetime is spent in a wealthy family or a very poor one. It does not care whether the body is beautiful and healthy or ugly and crippled. All it cares about is what lessons are learned consciously so that when a particular lifetime is completed, spiritual progress will have been made. This does not mean that the soul is unfeeling for, as part of God, the soul is pure love and bliss. But the soul fully realizes that these characteristics of rich or poor, healthy or sick, are only illusions and are not real. The soul is concerned only with utilizing the appearances of these illusions to achieve eternal conscious growth in what is beyond illusion.

LIFE IS A SCHOOL

This can help in better understanding what appear to be cruel accidents of fate in the world around us. Imagine the kind of life experience that awaits a baby conceived in the womb of a drug-addicted mother. From the first moment of incarnation at conception, the embryo is being fed toxins and contaminants instead of healthy blood and other nutrients. He is a drug addict, himself, at birth and usually will have little or no healthy support from mother or family. This apparent tragedy tears at the heartstrings and it is easy to understand why people often ask, "Why does God allow such calamities?" Part of the answer is that the incarnating soul enters the new baby body solely for the purpose of learning. If one's belief is that we each have one lifetime only, then such an unfortunate circumstance would seem grossly unfair. Awareness that a soul returns to embodiment as many times as necessary to learn all needed lessons can bring great comfort. When my husband was stricken in 1978, I felt I might literally have grieved myself to death had it not been for my awareness that he would have other opportunities in another lifetime. While this faith did not prevent my grieving, it did alleviate some of the despair I might have felt.

A soul reincarnates at the same level from which it left off in its last lifetime. If that person was a drug addict or dealer whose conduct contributed much pain and human suffering, how is he now going to teach himself to behave better? He was unwilling to consciously choose action that honored himself and other people in his last lifetime, and will probably only begin to learn if he experiences enough pain. When this soul is ready to reincarnate in yet another human body, the desire or craving for drugs still held at death will naturally propel him to seek conception in a womb where he can get drugs the fastest — the womb of an addicted mother — and he will be born addicted.

This does not mean that one should take a calloused attitude toward these unfortunate little ones. On the contrary, I feel great concern for them and for their spiritually sleeping parents. We must realize, however, that God as an almighty, separate Being has not sentenced a poor innocent victim to an unfair fate. Instead, it is the God essence in their own soul which has chosen this frightful experience so that eventually, when the pain becomes great enough, the person will begin to awaken to a more conscious, responsible way of living. Through repeated incarnations, the person will be led to awaken to his true identity as the soul and to God-life. Ralph Waldo Emerson referred to this as being "transhumanized into a God."

When you begin to see this overview, you realize that a person must follow the path he is on until he sees the wisdom of choosing differently. People who expend great amounts of energy attempting to get an addict or alcoholic to avoid the substance to which he is addicted finally may realize that only the addict, himself, can choose to change. The person who is trying to "save" that addict frequently does more harm than good, for his efforts may actually delay the addict's discovery that he is pursuing a dead-end road. It is one thing to attempt to serve an addicted person with information and support, and quite another to make it your job to rescue him. Ultimately, the greatest service you can render may be to step aside and allow him to make his own choices and reap any natural consequences that result therefrom.

When a child is very young, he may cry and feel totally abandoned because mother leaves the room. Because he cannot see her, he thinks she is gone forever. Likewise, at this present stage of evolution on earth, when a person of any age leaves the body, people frequently perceive him as being gone forever, instead of being aware that he has only left his physical form. In his book, Life After Life, Dr. Raymond Moody recounts numerous instances of persons in near-death experiences who did not want to return to physical earth life and chose to do so only because it served another person. If we glimpse what the other side is truly like, we will grieve only for our own loss when a loved one departs his physical body for a while, usually to wait for us in the wondrous light realms beyond this dimension.

EVOLUTION THROUGH FREE CHOICE

The Divine plan for liberation is through free choice. Free will is never taken away. You can take as many lifetimes as you choose to awaken. You have the power to make your own choices and select your own responses to each experience, whether or not you allow yourself consciously to be aware of how you go about the choosing. You can decide to feel victimized and helpless as a result of childhood experiences, or you can resolve to heal the wounds you may carry and then get on with your life, becoming stronger for having wrestled with the powerful opponent of adverse circumstances. Such wrestling can build great spiritual strength.

To most people, these concepts are lofty ones. Even when you can see from this expanded viewpoint, it is easy to lose sight of them, especially when raising a child, because we often think we must determine his life for him. The old model of psychology was that a newborn is a blank slate on which the parent could write anything. If this were really true, parenting would be an even more awesome responsibility than it actually is. Under this old model most good things the young one achieved were to the credit of the parents, and the blame for bad deeds was also laid at their doorstep. To make matters worse, many cultural and religious belief systems still teach that sex is sinful and that newborns, conceived in sin, are inherently dirty and require cleansing. What horrendous guilt and self-judgment mankind has needlessly taken upon itself with these false beliefs, no less harmful because they have no foundation in truth. Thankfully, this old psychological model is giving way to a much more expanded perspective.

RECOGNIZING THE DIVINITY IN A CHILD

A newborn is the return to embodiment of a mighty soul who knows what it needs to learn in order to continue its homeward journey. The most empowering way to deal with this little one is to recognize his divinity, and realize that the soul knows what it needs to do, what it needs to choose and what it needs to experience. A parent can be most empowering to his child by becoming spiritually attuned himself and providing guidelines that contain some flexibility. Giving a youngster the freedom to make his own mistakes (without so much latitude as to hurt himself irreparably) allows him to grow into a mature, successful person. A good rule of thumb is to treat a child the way you want God to treat you.

The soul within a young person usually will respond very positively when appealed to by a loving, spiritual parent who allows the child to comprehend the natural consequences of an action. With very young ones, this must be conveyed simply with few words. Children will usually not recall words, thoughts and ideas because they have not really begun to develop the mental nature yet, but they will never forget the energy of an experience. Nor are they fooled by a pretense, even when it is meant to reassure them, for children know exactly what is occurring essentially at the energy level of an interaction.

It is always best to be honest with a child. This does not mean giving explanations which are beyond his ability to understand, but a parent can be emotionally honest and a youngster will feel reassured because he already is feeling the emotional energy. When a little one experiences the emotional honesty of his parent, he feels reassured. His self-confidence grows as his trust of himself, his inner world and his ability to understand are validated.

As children, only a small portion of our internal experience is verified by those around us. This sets up an inner struggle: It is as though we have to choose what we will have — our inner experience or validation by others. Lack of validation is injurious to a child for he is attempting to align his own inner reality with the world he is discovering outside. If he becomes afraid, for instance, and everyone else pretends that there is nothing to fear, he will feel, additionally, that something may be wrong with himself because he feels afraid. On the other hand, with the same frightening event, if a parent validates his fearful feeling, the child will likely come to the conclusion that he is alright because his feelings are normal ones.

When parents feel too responsible for a child's life, the result is often that the child is deprived of valuable growth that can come only from making his own age-appropriate choices and, consequently, his own mistakes. Even as infants, we are powerfully creative, limitless beings. Only the little body is helpless and weak.

When a parent recognizes these truths, he can provide guidelines which will keep a young one safe as he grows and learns. The result for the child is autonomy and independence, which all healthy parents want for their children. The very nature of the soul, itself, is love, autonomy and power. Indeed, a portion of God could never be less.

> "Our birth is but a sleep and a forgetting
> The soul that rises with us, our life's star
> Hath had elsewhere its setting
> And cometh from afar
> Not in entire forgetfulness
> And not in utter nakedness
> But trailing clouds of glory do we come
> From God, who is our home."
> William Wordsworth

THE HUMAN TAPESTRY

Insight into the cosmic order is synchronous with insight into the deepest levels of human nature. In the great tapestry of human life each person enters each incarnation afresh, bringing with him certain patternings which comprise the template for lessons he must learn in order to continue his spiritual evolution. After arrival again in a human body, each free choice either clears some of the complexity already existing or adds further complexity, which will remain until the patterning is dissolved. Another way to say this is that by a person's actions, the mountain of lessons to be learned is either growing or shrinking.

In the giant weaving of a life, there are many knottings which function like glitches in the energy of the person. These may be the result of traumas to the psyche in this incarnation or in past incarnations. There usually seem, however, to be only a few primary knots. When a primary knot is released and its energy absorbed, experienced and thus integrated, it dissolves, and any secondary knottings are simultaneously removed. These subsidiary knots have only come into existence as a way to provide another view of that original, primary energy pattern, thus allowing a glimpse from a different perspective.

The soul is relentless in its efforts to bring you into attunement with itself. It keeps trying, keeps providing yet another view from yet another perspective until, sooner or later, you begin to see more than the material the knot plays itself out on. You eventually begin to notice that an energy pattern which is forming yet another knot on yet another new material is a familiar pattern you have seen before. You realize that this new drama in your life is really some old drama that is being acted out by different players. The costumes, the scenery and the actors are different, but this is the same old script. Sometimes this is expressed this way:

"My father abused me while I was little, then I grew up and my boyfriend abused me. I broke up with him and later got married and my husband abused me."

Such entanglements can reveal patterns that have been repeated throughout a whole lifetime. As heartbreaking as life's disappointments can be, you will ultimately arrive at the realization that all pain can be alleviated. You will have as many lifetimes as you require to become completely whole. Whether you arrive at a healed stage through the advantages which would be present in ideal life and family circumstances or through the self-effort of congruently taking up the work of your own healing, you will ultimately arrive at the portal of spiritual life. When the light of Spirit penetrates sufficiently into your life, it begins to heal whatever traumas may remain, purifying and readying you to live in attunement with the soul.

12

Fullness of Joy

When you open yourself to the highest inspirations, a power and creativity will flow through you that will never fail to uplift and encourage. When you close the door to the higher energy, you deprive yourself as well as the world.
Christina Thomas

The secret of success in any endeavor is to unite your outward expression with the power within. The entire self-conscious world encourages and supports mediocrity, but work inspired by the soul is always excellent in the result it achieves, for it is not possible to overestimate God. You are here to interact with this divine energy at every moment, responding to its inspiration. A desultory life could be likened to a field of poor soil, which will yield a scanty crop. Once that life is cleansed and spiritualized, the soil becomes richly fertile, and any seed planted therein will grow and produce prolifically.

THE SOUL'S EXPRESSION IS UNIQUE

The manifestation of the soul is always original. Comparison is of little value for the soul always creates anew, seeing the utter perfection of each created being. Utilize another's excellent performance as an inspiring model in your chosen line of work, but never disparage yourself or your results - or those of another - through unfavorable comparison. When you compete, you may block the artistry of your soul, which can weave the threads of your life into a masterful, original tapestry. The highest purpose of your presence in bodily form is to function in alignment with the might of the soul. When you do this, your work will be magnificent and your happiness will seem boundless. If you are not experiencing this fullness of joy, the lack, itself, can be a signal to look in a different place. There is a song the soul wants to sing through you, a poem it wants to write, a person it wants to hug or a landscape it wants to paint. It matters not that whatever you long to do has been done a thousand times. The creative energy in your life is waiting to express its unique joy and until you have responded to the soul's boundless expression, your world is incomplete. Ask your soul to direct you, today, toward its magic.

FINDING YOUR OWN UNIQUE EXPRESSION

If you are an artist, then to the extent that you open yourself to the power of the soul will your paintings be inspired instead of ordinary. Because their source lies in the etheric realms of the superconscious, the images in your art will reflect a sense of joy to others and will help to stimulate their own unique creativity.

Are you a writer? Then, to the degree that you feel the aliveness of the soul as you pour your thoughts and ideas onto paper, will your words carry a vibration of love, striking a resonant chord deep within your readers. Information, alone, could never accomplish the healing and upliftment which results from a manuscript so energized. Such a book has a life of its own, lasting long after others are out of print. It is treasured by its readers for the feeling of comfort and restorative energy which it imparts, much as a crystal augments the power in a radio.

One who writes out of expediency will never tap the power known by the amanuensis of the soul. Such an inspired scribe never knows writer's block, for ideas, images and revelations present themselves faster than his pen can fly across the page. Neither is the success of book sales a primary concern, for the time spent in writing contains its own joyful reward. When you lose your self in the work at hand, you discover the True Self you have always sought.

Do your talents lie outside the arts? Have you judged and underestimated yourself, thinking that you have no talent at all? It is important to know that regardless of how your hands are busied at the moment, if the soul's vibrant energy is allowed to flow through, all activity is worthwhile and valuable.

If you are a mother tending a small child, you will gather additional strength for your day when you recognize that Divine Mother is nurturing you as you care for your child. At exasperating moments, quietly turn within for support and a stream of sustenance will infuse your awareness, like a cool breeze on a humid day, and your patience will extend beyond its usual limits.

In the role of nurturer more than any other, it is vital to ask God's partnership in your endeavor. If you function from the battery of your own stored-up reserve, you are sure to exhaust yourself. Mothering is one of the most important occupations on earth. It is not even a slight exaggeration to say that as you care for little ones, you share in shaping the future of humankind. A mother literally creates and holds the major part of the context, for good or ill, of the new lives entrusted to her care. The most important treasure a very small child can have is a strong, spiritual mother who loves him unconditionally.

Are you a speaker? To the degree that you give the real work of effective communication to the genius within will your presence be a welcome treat. It is certainly worthwhile to spend diligent time in preparation, but make it your primary intent to stimulate and acknowledge the people assembled, rather than focus attention on yourself. When your goal is to touch and empower each listener, self-consciousness will quickly drop away, and you will feel a great surging increase of energy. As a warm spring shower softens the ground and soaks into the earth around tiny roots to spur a burst of growth in young plants, your words will bring a recharging aliveness to your audience. The minutes or hours allocated for your presentation will fly by. Afterward, those gathered to hear you will feel more relaxed and invigorated than when your talk began and your services will be in high demand.

DISCONTENTED WITH YOUR JOB?

Do you dislike your job or your employer? You can engage one of the most potent tools available if you begin to treat your employer as God and your present job as the assignment given you for your spiritual growth by a great master teacher. When you live with this attitude, your soul can quickly teach you any required lessons and you then may be released to perform activities more to your liking. This principle works in all areas. If you find unpleasant aspects in your life, use this technique sincerely and watch how quickly your circumstances change. Your soul is not interested in punishing you; it just wants you to wake up. When you begin to work consciously with the elements in your daily life, taking full responsibility for each unpleasantness as a way to begin changing it, you will find a great speeding up of your spiritual progress.

CHOOSING PEACE IN EACH MOMENT

Many people think that happiness is a result of reaching some tangible goal regardless of how it is gained. Denying the spiritual aspect of their own lives, such persons may secretly harbor turbulent, misery-producing emotions, which actually create and perpetuate unhappiness. Inner peace could be compared to a handful of seeds which, planted in fertile soil, will produce an abundant crop of good feelings. Just as you would not expect a fragrant lilac bush to grow where some stinkweed seeds had been buried in the ground, to look for happiness as an outgrowth of discordant feelings is to place an order for disappointment. In order to reap the happy results you want in your life, choose today to plant seeds of peace in all circumstances.

You may feel that you have too much work in the everyday world to allow your creativity to be expressed, but you will never be truly happy until you balance this with your inner need for creative expression. All activity, whether mundane or ethereal, is creative when the power of the soul flows through it. Finding this expression and the balance needed to live congruently in your life is the ongoing challenge and reward of the spiritual journey.

There is a story from ancient India which provides a wonderful model for finding this balance between material life and attunement with the soul and its creative expression. King Janaka, who was also a great saint, summoned a disciple who had qualified for his next initiation.

"Your assignment," said King Janaka to the chela, "is to go through each room of my palace and pay such complete attention to each detail, that when you are done, you will have memorized every detail of every room." Each room of the vast palace was enormous and so elaborately furnished with jewels, gold, rich tapestries and rare treasures that the inventory of even one chamber would be a challenge to remember. The Saint-King continued with the assignment, "One further challenge is that you are to carry with you at all times a teaspoon filled to the brim with oil ... and never spill a drop!"

In this metaphor, the vast palace with all its many, elaborate rooms represents the journey through life with all its complexities and distractions. The teaspoon is your "center" — that place of stillness within you which is established through consistent practice in meditation. The oil is the awareness of the divine presence - awareness of the soul deep within. If your attention is too engrossed in the outer world with its quixotic highs and lows, you will spill the oil. On the other hand, if you focus solely on the oil to the neglect of the outer world, you may not perform the functions your soul wants you to achieve this lifetime. Balance, therefore, is always the desirable way.

Never before has such a model been more desperately needed, for society in general and human beings in particular are undergoing many changes. The crying need for authentic values and a faith that can stand against the storm is glaringly apparent all over the world. The old ways which worked adequately in the past for both individuals and societies work no longer. We are already well into the transition between the old way and the new. Political boundaries are now shifting so rapidly that last month's newspaper may well be more current than any available world map. Simultaneously, the enormous challenges in the lives of millions of human beings is beyond the scope of anything in recorded history. The urgent need for an inner stability has already reached a critical point throughout our world.

Although these are, indeed, very perilous times, they, perhaps, can best be viewed in the light of the Chinese symbol for crisis, which is a combined form representing a balance of opportunity and danger. Peril seems to exist in all transformation and transition, yet change is the only constant we know, without which there is no growth. The rapid worldwide pace of shifting boundaries today is often bewildering to the individual. Yet the challenge of change and transformation, of mundane activity and inspired creativity can and must be met and dealt with by the individual in his own life. Caterpillars transform into butterflies one at a time!

A technique, which I call my "view from eternity," helps me achieve inner balance during both highs and lows. When faced with any decision, life situation, threat or opportunity about which I feel any uncertainty, I imagine that I have just left my body at the end of this incarnation and that I am standing with the Being of Light reviewing choices made during this lifetime. I then ask, "What will I be glad I chose to do from this viewpoint?" Invariably, I immediately know the choice my soul wants to make and can proceed more harmoniously.

In India it is customary to greet others by pressing the palms together lightly, bowing the head and saying, "Namaste," a Sanskrit word which means, "I bow to the God in you." On achieving reunion with the soul, one realizes how this lovely custom probably originated. It is a dignified expression of reverence and a reminder each time it is used that each of us is essentially divine.

It is a blessing to interact with each other on this stage of life. As I envision this great whirling globe of Mother Earth spinning in space, carrying all of us wearing different costumes and acting out our various roles, I feel tremendous gratitude for the privilege of communicating directly from my heart in this way. Wherever you are as you read these words, I honor the divinity within you.

Namaste.

It May Be Helpful to Remember . . .

1. The Soul is God individualized. The Soul is your essence.
2. Your human parents gave you a physical body and the chance to grow up in a family. This is wonderful service and it is appropriate to honor and be grateful for the great opportunity to be in human form, but you do not have to be burdened for life by belief systems that no longer work for you if you choose to do the necessary inner healing work.
3. Your real parent (and true identity) is light, love and energy.
4. The divine plan for evolution is through free will.
5. Each of us is 100% responsible for our own experiences.
6. The soul reincarnates repeatedly in human form until the individual realizes his conscious identity as a child of God.
7. You will have as many lifetimes as needed to accomplish this.
8. You *have* a body, mind and personality but you are not the body, mind or personality. You are Spirit, energy - the Soul.
9. The ultimate purpose of life is conscious reunion with the soul.
10. In addition, there is a unique *individual* purpose for your life. When you remember it, you will have found your work and will then experience unparalleled clarity, peace and dedication.
11. You will remember your unique soul purpose for this lifetime when you get in touch with the energy of the Soul.
12. The true purpose of the ego is to protect the physical body and be the obedient servant of the Soul.
13. There is no eternal hell. You cannot be lost.
14. The only way out of the cycles of reincarnation is by graduation to the Super Conscious level.
15. It is safe to be alive and make mistakes, for that is how we learn.
16. God is not angry. God is Love.
17. You can trust your Soul to guide you to your next right step.

Glossary

addiction - the state of being given up or having yielded to a habit or practice or to something that is habit-forming, as narcotics, to such an extent that its cessation causes severe trauma. A giving over, surrender.

Ajna Chakra - Sixth of the Seven Primary Chakras. Located at the midspot between the eyebrows. A powerful, spiritual center of will and focus.

amanuensis - A person employed to write what another dictates.

Avatar - A being who is God in form. From "ava" (Sanskrit), meaning "to come down."

Babaji - Deathless Mahavatar of India. For more, read "Autobiography of a Yogi," by Paramahansa Yogananda. The title "Babaji" means "Revered Father." (Sanskrit).

Bhagavad-Gita - "The Song of God" (Sanskrit). A segment of the Mahabbharata, sacred scripture of India.

bhajan(s) - devotional songs or chants (Sanskrit).

The "Big Movie" - Approximately one million years of earth life is required to evolve from the first stage of human life (self-consciousness) to the first stage of God life (Superconsciousness). Time spent in disease or addiction produces no forward motion and the years thus necessary to accomplish the requisite spiritual maturity may actually be closer to two million. If an average lifespan of 75 years is considered, many thousands of lifetimes will be consumed in this transit. These repeated incarnations utilize many different living dramas played out on the stage of Schoolhouse Earth, wherein we gradually learn through experience to make choices that will finally result in our reunion with the soul. When one fully matures into Superconsciousness, he realizes that these dramas are illusions. Like movies, they seem real but are only light images being played out on the screen of each individual life. For more, see "Autobiography of a Yogi" and "Cosmic Consciousness."

chakras - The seven primary energy centers located (at the astral level) in the brain and along the spinal column of a human being.

chela - disciple (Sanskrit).

Christ - One who has evolved to the plane of Super Consciousness and who is fully identified with the Soul.

connected breathing - Usually refers to Rebirthing.

embodiment - An incarnation.

ecstasy - Mental transport or rapture from the contemplation of divine things.

ego - 1. The "I" or self of any person; a person as thinking, feeling and willing and distinguishing itself from the selves of others and from objects of its thought. (Random House Dictionary)
2. For purposes of this book, "ego" is used to mean that separate part of the conscious mind which is not connected to the genius and power of the soul until sufficient evolution in consciousness occurs within the person.

genius - An exceptional natural capacity of intellect, especially as shown in creative and original work in art, music. Strong inclination. Guardian spirit.

gnosis - Knowledge of spiritual things; mystical knowledge.

hologram - 1. A negative produced by exposing a high-resolution photographic plate, without camera or lens, near a subject illuminated by monochromatic, coherent radiation, as from a laser: when placed in a beam of coherent light a true three-dimensional image of the subject is formed. 2. A three-dimensional image without physical substance. A light image. There are theories that the entire universe is a hologram. For more, read "The Holographic Universe," by Michael Talbot.

incarnation - A lifetime in a physical body.
(From Latin "incarnat" meaning "made flesh")

Jesus - The first person in this present cycle of recorded history to fully embody Super Consciousness.

karma - The law of cause and effect. In modern terms, a colloquial expression of this would be "what goes around, comes around." Conveys the understanding that all actions must be compensated and thus balanced.

Kriyaban - An individual who is initiated into and who practices the technique of Kriya Yoga in meditation. May also be called "Kriya Yogi."

Kriya Yoga - An ancient simple psycho-physiological connected breathing technique which greatly speeds up human evolution through a direct burning away of karma. Mahavatar Babaji reintroduced it to the modern world in 1861. For more, read "Autobiography of a Yogi," by Paramahansa Yogananda, Self-Realization Fellowship, Publishers.

Mahavatar - Great Avatar. Maha = Great (Sanskrit)

mantra - A sound or set of sounds, often used to open certain energy centers (usually temporarily). A mantra is a "seed sound."

mystic - A person who attains insight into mysteries transcending ordinary human knowledge by immediate intuition in a state of spiritual ecstasy.

Namaste - Sanskrit term meaning "I bow to the God in you" or, sometimes, "I bow to the Light in you."

numen - Divine power or spirit, deity.

numinous - Of, pertaining to, or like a numen; spiritual or supernatural. Surpassing comprehension or understanding. Mysterious; that element in artistic expression which remains numinous. Arousing one's elevated feelings of duty, honor, loyalty, devotion, commitment, passion.

nurturometer - That inner measurement of one's need for nurturing including both quality and quantity. This is always unique to the individual and is valid without comparison or outside measurement. A child, for instances, needs to be nurtured as much as *he* needs nurturing.

paradigm - An example; pattern.

perturbation - Great emotional, psychological (and sometimes physical) agitation, occurring at times of great stress and usually preceding a quantum leap to a higher level of consciousness in a transformational experience.

preternatural - Supernatural.

rebirthing - A method of connected breathing used to clear emotional, physical and psychological suppressions of energy.

reincarnation - Rebirth of the soul in another human form. Literally means "in flesh again."

sacred space - A temporary state of consciousness, usually accessed as a result of tremendous feeling. Often used to describe a person who is intensely grieved over the loss of a loved one.

Sanskrit - Precedent tongue of all Indo-European languages. Has been in existence for many thousands of years. Made up of "seed sounds" (bija), meaning that whole chunks of knowledge and awareness are embodied in single words or phrases. Seed sounds, when heard, spoken or chanted, cause latent knowingness to be released from within the brain, whether or not the conscious mind has understanding of how this occurs, in much the same way that a seed, under proper conditions, releases the flowering plant it always contained in potentiality.

Super Consciousness - The infinite realm beyond the zone of self-consciousness.

transmigration of the soul - After reaching the human (self-conscious) level, a soul reincarnates only in human forms, except in rare instances. If a person uses his God-given free will to choose to engage in bestial or other behavior not befitting a human, he may revert to the animal level for one lifetime only in order to learn not to behave in such lowly ways. This accounts for the instances of exceptionally intelligent horses or dogs. After having lived even one lifetime as a human, such an embodiment in animal form would be so painful and limiting that the needed lessons would be learned.

transpersonal - Expanded beyond the personal.

True Self - The Soul. The real identity of a human being beyond the limitation of physical life.

Universal Energy Field - The sea of universal energy which is within and all around you.

yoga - Literally "yoke" (Sanskrit) or union. Refers to practice of specific discipline(s) to unify diversant energies and focus them toward the highest goal of union with the divine. "Take my yoke upon you...." (Matthew 11:29)

Yogananda, Paramahansa - The first great spiritual master from India to live in the United States for an extended period of time. Chosen by Babaji to bring the liberating technique of Kriya Yoga to the west. Founder of Self-Realization Fellowship.

yogi - One who practices yoga (feminine form = yogini).

Logo of the Inner Light Institute. Symbolizes attaining the light of Spirit through the love of the heart. A devotee, whose calm inner gaze in deep meditation is focused on the Ajna Chakra (also called the Christ Center) located at the mid-spot between the eyebrows, sees a radiant, five-pointed star pulsating in a dark background, encircled by a ring of vibrant light. Telescoping his consciousness through this star, he moves through the Christ Center to Cosmic Consciousness.

Index

Index

I believe that there is nothing new in the Universe -- only new *discoveries* of what has always existed. Life, itself, is a school with many subjects to cover and master in order to graduate. The next right step for you, therefore, may be different than for another person. It is important to tune in to the direction of your own soul for unique, personal guidance. If you are honestly seeking the Light, you will be guided all along the way, whether or not it is apparent. When we realize that loving, unseen assistance is always present, the journey becomes easier.

It is my joy and pleasure to share with you this perspective of ancient truths which have been revealed to me through the writings of other sincere, devoted people and through inner personal revelation. My heart's desire is that this book will serve you to become more awakened to the power and magnificence of your true nature.

Books

SECRETS
A Practical Guide to Undreamed-Of Possibilities

Contents

A PRACTICAL GUIDE TO UNDREAMED-OF POSSIBILITIES.

SECRETS

Christina Thomas

"After distancing myself from the dogmatism of the fundamental religion in which I was raised, I sought answers to nagging spiritual questions. I could not reconcile the inner spiritual love I felt with the narrowness and nonacceptance of the church. Although I half believed their fearful warnings that if I left to seek light in my own way I would be doomed, I left anyway, trusting that God would guide me. Groping through the darkness to find spiritual and psychological wholeness, I looked for a model to follow and often thought, 'somebody ought to write a book about this,' not knowing that I would be that 'somebody.' Here I have written about that quest and the Secrets, both miraculously effective and extraordinarily practical, which brought more joy and peace into my life than I ever dreamed of."   Christina Thomas

A model for wholeness. Full of Love.

ISBN#0-9622119-0-7   220 pages   #1 $9.95

Audio Cassettes

SECRETS

The most powerful Secret of All is that Thought is Creative. When you focus your attention in this powerful, directed way, you create the new life you want. Includes actual processes for Centering, Relaxation, Concentration, Creating your Ideal Day, Creating a Time Warp, Telepathic Communication and Drowning Out Negative Chatter. Many people use this tape to make powerful, positive life changes.   45 mins. #2 $9.95

REBIRTHING: Heal Your Life

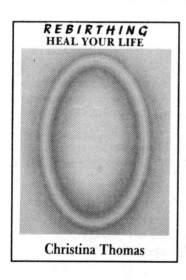

Profound and practical, this tape provides potent explanation, real-life examples and clear insight regarding using your natural breathing to clear long-stored suppressions of guilt, regret, anger and fear so you can feel the vibrant joy of today. Once cleared of this burden of static, you will experience a life filled with love, enthusiasm and creativity springing forth from within. Awakening, informative and evocative. 1 hour #3 $9.95

Audio Cassettes

HEAL YOUR INNER CHILD

Journey from one year prior to your birth, experiencing that YOU were fully aware even before conception. Discover how, through infancy and early childhood, you acquired an accumulation of emotional and psychological baggage which you can now discard in order to live more fully and freely than you may imagine. Just as one can enter graduate school without finding fault with any beliefs he or she had in fifth grade, you can now clear the slate to begin the next phase of your life without being held back by limiting thoughts.

Recorded live during REBIRTHING SCHOOL at INNER LIGHT INSTITUTE

HEAL YOUR INNER CHILD

Christina Thomas

Recorded live during
Rebirthing School at Inner Light Institute

2-tape program includes in-depth, live discussion of

- How we numb our aliveness to fit into a family
- Breathing through to purpose, power, abundance.
- How to identify and change your family patterns
- How to integrate suppressed energy **as it arises**
- Achieving wholeness within yourself
- Moving beyond the mind to authentic power
- Balancing feminine/masculine for a happier life
- Discovering your soul purpose for this life
- Healing and honoring your little inner child

75 minutes 2-Cassette Program #4 $12.95

Audio Cassettes

IN TUNE WITH THE SOUL

Christina Thomas

A summarized version of the book spoken by the author.

Deals with vital, life-changing issues and processes in an inspired and personal manner. Tap into the pure gold at the center of your being.

45 minutes   #5 $9.95

Your Soul Purpose

Christina Thomas

On this cassette, Christina focuses on identifying and engaging in the activity your soul longs to do.

When you discover Your Soul Purpose, you will experience a sense of passion, dedication, commitment and creative excellence unparalleled by any person functioning in a mediocre way. Attunement with the soul always calls forth a unique creativity from within each person. This tape helps you head toward your highest expression.

45 minutes   #6 $9.95

Order Form

Qty.	Item No.	Item	Price	Amount

Please use a blank sheet if more order space is needed

Please include shipping & handling charges:
$2.00 first item, 75c for each additional item
$3.00 for Priority Mail

Subtotal	
Shipping	
TOTAL	

____ Please send your Free Newsletter.

Name: (Please Print) _____

Address _____

City_____State_____ZIP _____

Telephone (   ) Day_____ Night_____

For   □ VISA   □ MASTERCARD orders only:

Card #_____ Exp.Date ————

Signature ——————————————————————

Checks payable and Mail to: **Chela Publications**
977 Seminole Trail, Suite 308
Charlottesville, VA 22901 • USA
Credit Card Orders (804) 961-2960

List of Workshops

Secrets of Mastery

In Tune With The Soul

Dynamics of Communication

The Firewalk Experience

Rebirthing School

Seven-Day Healing Intensive

Miracles Now!

Ordering Information:

Books: #1 $9.95   SECRETS:
A Practical Guide to Undreamed-of Possibilities

#7 $10.95   IN TUNE WITH THE SOUL

Audio Cassettes:

#2 $9.95   SECRETS

#3 $9.95   REBIRTHING: Heal Your Life

#4 $12.95   HEAL YOUR INNER CHILD

#5 $9.95   IN TUNE WITH THE SOUL

#6 $9.95   YOUR SOUL PURPOSE

Order Form

Qty.	Item No.	Item	Price	Amount

Please use a blank sheet if more order space is needed

Please include shipping & handling charges:
$2.00 first item, 75c for each additional item
$3.00 for Priority Mail

Subtotal	
Shipping	
TOTAL	

_____ Please send your Free Newsletter.

Name: (Please Print) _____

Address _____

City_____State_____ZIP _____

Telephone (   )_Day_____Night_____

For   □ VISA   □ MASTERCARD orders only:

Card #_____ Exp.Date ————

Signature ——————————————————————

Checks payable and Mail to: **Chela Publications**
977 Seminole Trail, Suite 308
Charlottesville, VA 22901 • USA
(804) 961-2960
        Credit Card Orders :

What people are saying ...

"Your message is powerful and healing. I support your vision."
Philip Kavanaugh, M.D., *Pathway to Recovery*

" . . . most empowering experience of my life."
Rory Elder, Psychotherapist and Trainer

". . . created a powerful turning point for me, giving me a sense of connectedness and helping me to be in touch with my Higher Self. If more people could experience this, our Courts would be less crowded."
Honorable John Colton, Criminal Court Judge

"Thomas combines instruction and personal revelation in a balance which serves to cultivate hope and a willingness to attempt the journey."
Patricia D'Encarnacao, M.D., *Recovery Times*